YEARNING FOR EDEN

A SPIRITUAL JOURNEY TOWARD RE-CONNECTEDNESS, ROOTS, AND MEANING

Rev. Ernest Dyson, Ed.D.

Credits - Cover image Helen Marie Ramsey (Virginia)

Copyright Rev. Ernest Dyson, Ed.D., 2012

All Rights Reserved

DEDICATION

To the glory of God --

    The font of all knowledge and love.

To all those who have been my teachers --

    Both within and without the classroom.

Take my yoke upon you and learn from me, for I am gentle and humble in heart, and you will find rest for your souls (Matthew 11:29)[1]

---

[1] All Scripture quotations are from the New International Version unless otherwise noted.

ACKNOWLEDGEMENTS

The author would like to recognize four people who graciously gave their time and expertise to make this work a reality; without which this book would not have come to fruition. They all worked pro bono just in a desire to help. Their self-giving and encouragement reflect what this book is all about. For whatever contribution its message may make, they deserve a large share. All I had to do was write the book!

Helen Marie Ramsey, my loving and devoted companion, is responsible for pushing me time and time again to "Finish the manuscript," Are you working on your manuscript?" She is the artist whose work forms the background and final design of the cover.

Elaine Lewis, a gracious friend, is responsible for all the leg work that went into investigating the ins-and-outs of today's procedures for publishing. She kept insisting, "This manuscript has to be published," and would not give up finding a way to do it.

Don Fowler, a new and good friend, was responsible for all the technical work – formatting, walking me through a final print version draft, hours of manuscript revision, advice and knowledge of publishing procedures, and so much more. His "knowhow" aided in making the final work a reality.

Hank Altiman, a retired journalist and editor, edited the manuscript and made invaluable suggestions that improved the presentation you will read. His training and experience contributed significantly to the final product.

Thank you,

Ernest Dyson
September 15, 2012

> But while realizing their separateness
> They remain strangers, because they
> have not yet learned to love each other.
> ...The deepest need of man, then, is the
> need to overcome his separateness, to
> leave the prison of his aloneness.
>
> - Erich Fromm

CONTENTS

PART 1: WE'RE IN A MESS   1

CHAPTER 1: WE'RE IN THIS TOGETHER   2
- LOOKING WITHIN   6
- A STATE OF BEING   8
- INDIVIDUALITY   9
- MUTUALITY   11
- LIFTING OUR SIGHTS   13
- SOME VALUABLE VALUES   15

CHAPTER 2: AND WE'RE ALIENATED   31
- INSIDE A DEPRESSION   32
- THE UNCONNECTED FAMILY   34
- THE UNCONNECTED CHILD   37
- GOOD PEOPLE CAN DO BAD THINGS   39
- TOGETHER BUT APART   42
- STRANGERS IN A LONELY CROWD   46
- THE FABRIC OF LIFE   48
- THE LOSS OF SELF   51
- THE LOSS OF SOUL   53

PART II: BUT WE'RE CONNECTED TO A COSMOS   55

CHAPTER 3: NATURE'S DANCE   56

CONNECTION AND FEELING GOOD	56
A SYMBIOTIC SYSTEM	59
ORDER IN DISORDER	63
NATURE'S NECESSITY	67

CHAPTER 4: THE MEANING OF THE DANCE — 70

ANCIENT WISDOM	71
SCIENCE AND FAITH	73
YOU, ME, AND THE WHOLE UNIVERSE	76
A GOOD THING TURNED BAD	77
FREE WILL AND LOVE	79
A "CATCH 22"	80

PART III: AND WE'RE CONNECTED TO THE DIVINE — 84

CHAPTER 5: UNDERSTANDING IT — 85

IMAGES THAT PLAY IN THE MIND	87
PICTURING THE SELF	89
PICTURING THE MIND	91
MADE IN THE IMAGE OF LOVE	93
DISCOVERING AN OBJECT LOST	97
WHERE'S THE PROOF?	98
DENYING THE CONNECTION	101

CHAPTER 6: BELIEVING IT — 103

THE NECESSITY OF CONVICTION	104
THE FOUNDATION OF CONVICTION	105
BELIEF MAKES A DIFFERENCE	106

> LESSONS FROM ANOTHER REALM — 107

PART IV: WE'RE ALSO CONNECTED TO ETERNITY — 112

CHAPTER 7: ABOUT LIFE AND DEATH — 113
- SOMETHING OLD, NOT NEW — 116
- LIFE HANGS ON — 119
- BUT WHAT ABOUT DEATH? — 120
- A DEATH THAT IS FINAL MAKES NO SENSE — 124
- THEN WHERE DO WE GO FROM HERE? — 126

CHAPTER 8: SOME SPIRITUAL GEOGRAPHY — 128
- HEAVEN ON EARTH — 130
- ADJUSTING TO A NEW GEOGRAPHY — 136
- THE SPIRITUAL CONNECTION — 138
- WE ARE NOT APES — 140
- CHILDREN OF THE LIGHT — 146

PART V: SO WE CAN GET OUT OF THE MESS — 150

CHAPTER 9: REMAKING THE CONNECTION — 151
- WHAT "REAL" LOOKS LIKE — 152
- LOOKING OUTWARD — 154
- REACHING OUT TO TOUCH — 158
- FORGIVENESS THROUGH COMPASSION — 161
- A PARADIGM FOR PARDON — 164
- LIVING TOGETHER IN COMMUNITY — 166
- AN ANCIENT AND A MODERN EXAMPLE — 169
- THE SURRENDER OF WILL — 171

LIVING WITH AN ABIDING PRESENCE	173
CHAPTER 10: ACCEPTING	**176**
INVITATION	178
ACCEPTING THE GIFT OPENS THE GATE	179
RETURNING TO LOVE	181
COVENANT	184
THE LOVE FEAST	186
BE STILL AND KNOW	188
SHALOM	190
NOTES	**192**

INTRODUCTION

I am a counselor. I work with people who are experiencing traumatic emotional upset. Clients often come with the questions Doreen had. When I first met her, her pain was evident in her eyes, in her facial expression, in her body language and in the tone of her voice. "Why am I feeling this way?" she asked? "Why am I so irritable and angry all the time? Why can't I sleep through the night without rolling and tossing? What is wrong with me?" Doreen was in the throes of a clinical depression, and we would have to work at finding what the roots of that were to help her rectify what was causing her upset.

I remember being told by a teacher when I was a youngster that the quality of "genius" was the ability to see into the center of things and reduce them to their simplest component. And I believe that is so. For when we can sweep away the complicating entanglements and peripheries of any situation, problem, or system we are in a position to deal with those phenomena in more effective ways. When science can uncover the fundamental process of disease, for example, then treatments for prevention, control, or cure become possible. When the court is able to get to the core of truth involved in a dispute, justice can follow. When a couple can be helped to understand the basic issues involved in their marital difficulties, then they are in a position to build a healthier relationship.

In the same way, if we can identify the quintessential principle from which life is designed to unfold, and apply that in our living, then our daily lives can be healthier, happier, and more fulfilling. When we look at the reflections we have of our society as portrayed in the media we see that there is a great deal of sickness, unhappiness, and unfulfilled desires in our individual and community lives. An often heard cry is that we need to return to "family values." We seem to have lost some standards that served us well in the past. There is a significant body of scientific research to indicate that there are basic values that support our individual, family, and societal well-being.

We sense that something is amiss in life. The apprehension grows out of the lack of satisfaction we feel in the things that we do from day to day. It is evidenced by our sleeplessness; our increasing dependence on drugs, both prescribed and illicit; the boredom we try to obliterate by filling life with possessions; the emptiness that we try to fill with the trivia of television; the overemphasized concern with sexual gratification; a soaring divorce rate; the abuse that runs rampant in our families; the lack of communication with our teenagers; the violence of our society -- and the list could go on.

Is there a basic principle, a core insight about life that we could find if we were able to unravel the complications and intricacies of living together? Is there a "genius" perspective that if understood would guide our daily living and engender a different feeling about ourselves and what we do?

Could this erase the malaise and boredom that is often a part of modern living? Could it perhaps lift us to a new level of enjoyment, giving us a new sense of personal fulfillment and well-being? Could it change the character of our daily life? Could it provide a new zest to each day? Could it be the source of an energy that sustains us and sees us through the traumas of life that come to each one of us? Could such an insight, if acted upon, undergird us with an abiding personal happiness and lead us to a new sense of "family" and "community?"

I believe that life is a much simpler affair than we often understand it to be. And if we can see it in these simple terms our daily living can become less complicated, more assured, more comfortable, and more beautiful. We get so wrapped up in the day to day gratification of our personal needs and desires that we lose sight of a larger reality that engulfs our lives. As the old saw goes, "We can't see the forest for the trees."

This book is designed as a journey into insight that hopefully may change perception. It will not present a series of steps that guide to a promised conclusion, for life cannot be compartmentalized in that way. Instead its purpose is to unfold a simple understanding about "connection," which can become the basis for the reorientation of life for all those who wish to make the journey. As perception changes, the whole character of our day to day living changes.

To achieve this goal we must face the fact of our "disconnection." This alienation places us in contention with others and with a creation of which we are a keystone part. It has separated us from the spiritual aspects of our humanity and the eternal dimensions of life.

This disconnection produces upset. It is the root of the myriad mental and emotional problems that plague us as individuals. It prevents our gaining that deep sense of well-being that will quell the unrest that nags at us. It is the source of our societal ills. It accentuates the loneliness that is a part of the human condition. It creates a fear of the physical death which we all must face. It produces a distorted perception of who we are, what life is designed to be, where life has come from, and where life is headed. It makes a mess!

In the first four parts of the book we will unfold the insights related to these considerations. In the final section we will deal with the very practical matter of getting out of the mess, which will help individuals who are *Yearning for Eden*.

PART 1: WE'RE IN A MESS

> The real problem is in the hearts and minds of men. It is not a problem of physics but of ethics. It is easier to denature plutonium than to denature the spirit of man.
>
> — Einstein

CHAPTER 1:
WE'RE IN THIS TOGETHER

The boy was only a shaver of a fellow, five years old but with a mind that was as sharp as a tack. Although I knew his grandparents well, I had not had much contact with young Michael. I knew he was a child born out of wedlock. The teenaged father initially denied his parenthood and showed no interest in the boy; the girl was too young and self-centered to do the mothering that a young child requires. On this Sunday morning we both happen to be waiting in the church hallway, I've forgotten why, and we struck up a conversation.

As we chit-chatted, passing the time of our wait, the exchange was of casual, kid-centered interests. Until, that is, I asked Michael what he'd like to be when he was grown up. His answer would have liked to knock my socks off!

"I don't know what I want to be yet, I'm only five, but I know when I get bigger I'm going to hurt people!"

Wow! Where had that come from? When I collected myself sufficiently to respond I made the only reply that my shocked mind could hold. "Why do you want to hurt people when you get bigger?" I asked.

His answer came quickly and deliberately, as a thing previously thought out would do. "Because people have hurt me!"

Since that Sunday morning I have thought time and again about young Michael's plan to avenge his hurt. Lacking the parental love, attention, and affirmation that all of us need in our nurturing, and experiencing the deep sense of hurt that that void engendered, Michael was unwilling to relate to others with love. And unless something in his life experience happened to change this child, he would go through his days as a distorted facsimile of what he, and all of us, were created to be.

If we look at our society through the eyes of the media reports; through our addictions, phobias, and neuroses; through our boredom with our jobs, our responsibilities, and our routines; through our endless quest to have and to get; through the violence in our communities, our schools, and our families; through our intolerance, greed, and self-centeredness; through our inability to function cooperatively to address our common needs and live in peace on an individual, community, state, national, and international level; we can see that, like Michael, our personal and corporate life is a distorted facsimile of what it could to be.

It is not that we have all been born out of wedlock to teenage parents who were not yet ready to understand and provide the foundations for a healthy, fulfilled life in harmony with others. The problem is of a higher order than that. People are not living in a way that promotes mutual well-being. As a human species who cohabit this earth, we do not exhibit the ability to function together in a way that can engender and sustain an environment of peaceful co-existence.

And that reflects a dysfunction at every level of our living, individual, family, and community. In the midst of a world that has run amuck, you and I have a difficult time ordering life so as to find that personal peace that all of us desire. We want to feel secure, be happy, and enjoy an inner feeling of contentment and well-being. But we find that difficult to achieve because we are born into a family (humankind) that has not been able to nurture us in the ways of loving relationship.

Now this does not mean that we cannot love our family, our friends, our sweethearts. Normal, healthy individuals are able to give and receive love and, indeed, have a need to do so. But on the broader scale, it is difficult for us to love humankind. We hate the one who has harmed us, we are intolerant of those who are "different" from us, forgiveness is tough to give. We stereotype and look down upon. Our language is laced with "spick" and "kike" and "queer" and "nigger," epithets that are degrading and demeaning. We do not give like consideration to all: our society is layered and there is animosity and mistrust between groups. And whether we realize it or not -- and most of us don't seem to acknowledge it -- all of this impacts our personal life, and the peace and contentment we can enjoy from day to day. We are caught up in and are a part of this "stew."

Young Michael had lost touch with the loving part of his nature because he had been hurt. It seems humanity has lost touch with a part of itself. It is a part we do not consciously realize is gone, yet a loss that gnaws at our insides. We search desperately for that which will bring us a lasting happiness, a soul deep contentment the lack of which keeps us restless. We struggle with the reality of a world condition that tells us this kind of peace is but a dream.

But inside the heart-place of our being, in the most central core of what we are, there seems to be an obstinate insistence that will not release the vision. For we do not relinquish the hope. We continue to search. Perhaps it is a memory that is woven within the fabric of our nature that goads us on -- a memory that is only a wispy haze that fluctuates in intensity, no longer clear enough to fully grasp. Something we have lost, but not quite. We know it is there and somehow we know it is good.

The void seems apparent in a disharmony, an imbalance that keeps us just off center. That inability to be in harmony with all that we are a part of makes it impossible for us to achieve a sense of completion, of fulfillment, and of contentment. So no matter what we try to fill our living with, there is a nagging restlessness, a discontent. We continue to seek that which will satisfy us and bring about that full sense of inner personal peace.

And the ways and places in which we search are myriad. If I could just lose some weight. If I can build my physique. If I can just get that job. If I can find the right mate. If I could only get a this or that. If I can find who I really am. If I could just have more fun. If I could just get out of these circumstances. If I had more money. If I can do enough good in this life. And the litany of "ifs" is endless.

We search and seek and we pursue. We look to our gurus, our pundits, our religious mentors, our experts in this and that field. We try to fill life with pleasures, recreations, position, power, things. We purchase self-help literature. We think and plan our moves. And there is nothing wrong with the healthy pursuit of any of the above. But for many of us the problem is that we are searching with the wrong focus. Our sights are not aimed in the right directions. And that is so because the human family into which we are born has lost touch with who we really are, where we have come from, and what it is that we are a part of. Let me illustrate that fact with information from medical practice.

LOOKING WITHIN

Too often our search for that inner sense of peace and satisfaction is centered on what we can find "out there" and bring into our life. The bent has been on *getting* and *having*. But through the studies being done in the field of psychoneuroimmunology (the study of the interaction between the mind, the brain, and the immune system) we are finding that the real power over our life lies within us, not outside our person.

Mitchell L. Gaynor, M.D. is one of the most recent practicing physicians to note this phenomenon. In his book *Healing Essence* Dr. Gaynor, who specializes in the treatment of cancer, points us to an inner reality that has the power to heal. He documents findings that grow out of his medical practice when he writes,

> People who had *proved* their remarkable healing power by participating in their own recovery all had one thing in common: they had an awareness of their *soul, essence,* or *inner being* (I use these terms interchangeably)... And I learned from them that awareness of our essence -- awareness alone -- is enough to set the healing process in motion.[1]

And not only is the awareness of this presence beneficial, but lack of such awareness is detrimental. He points out that, "Living life without an awareness of it having a deeper, more meaningful purpose and truth may lead to a variety of maladies, from depression to physical illness."[2]

We get in touch with this inner being, not through focusing on something outside our self, but by opening our awareness to what is within us. Gaynor writes, "This kind of knowing and understanding is not attained through our eyes or our minds. Rather it is an understanding that comes through quiet meditation, when we allow ourselves to let go temporarily of who we think we are, and listen to what our essence is trying to tell us."[3]

This finding is not a new revelation, but a contribution to an old understanding. It is the teaching of ancient religions and philosophies. In the 1950's Norman Vincent Peale wrote of an aspect of it in his book *The Power of Positive Thinking*. More recently Bernie S. Siegel, a surgeon, writes of this power we have to heal ourselves in his book *Love, Medicine and Miracles*. In this book Siegel points out the amazing effect on our immune system that an attitude of loving relationship produces. Love, he observes as a scientist, heals!

We should be great self- healers, because human beings are born lovers. We should not need to be taught how to love, for our inner essence is love. That is what scripture teaches when it says that we are made in the image of God (Ex. 1:27). God, the Bible tells us, is the very definition of love (1 John. 4:8). From our very inner core, we are designed to give and receive love, even as God does.

But we have lost touch with our essence; we have been corrupted by selfishness, which is unloving. That distortion has introduced stress into our lives and stress, medical science knows, suppresses our immune system. Stress brings about illness, love promotes wellness.

A STATE OF BEING

What these realities point us to is an understanding that there is a certain modus operandi to our existence that promotes and advances life. That mode of living has a mystery about it, for we do not comprehend fully the process that is at work. What we do see is that something mystical is operative that produces results that go beyond our conscious abilities. The evidence we have indicates that this state of being involves connecting with a power that works in and through our humanity when we are open to it, and when we are together in a harmonic relationship that emanates from love.

So to find that inner peace and contentment that we can abide in daily, that sense that, in the longer haul, all is well with us no matter what our present circumstance, we must connect with a reality that goes beyond our own ability to create by getting, having, and manipulating. We must be able to see our life and our days in a broader context than simply the daily chores and routines we perform week in and week out. We must find that overarching sense of belonging that opens us to our inner essence, that lends legitimacy and purpose to what we do and the things that happen to us, that promotes our health and well-being. And living in that context involves two dimensions: individuality and mutuality.

INDIVIDUALITY

Living things are designed to grow. The seed, once unleashed by fertilization, and with the proper nourishing, bursts forth in a continuing process of becoming. All healthy life, yours and mine, is an unfolding dynamic which strives toward its goal of fulfillment. So at any stage of our living we, as healthy individuals, are in process, advancing, striving, pushing forward, unfolding.

There is something within us, some force, which all psychiatrists and psychologists observe that fuels this growth. We cannot pinpoint its location in our physical anatomy, but it is a presence whose existence we certify by the effects we observe. It propels us toward health and well-being, wholeness and contentedness. Some call it the soul, others "life force." It has been called our inner person, along with Dr. Gaynor we have already referred to it as our essence. Whatever its label, it is an energy that propels us forward, moving us to grow, to develop, to become.

Ray S. Anderson has written a helpful guide about this developmental process in his book *Don't Give Up On Me -- I'm Not Finished Yet*. In it he writes about our individual journey to become the person we were meant to be. Each of us is on a pilgrimage of self-actualization that seeks out health, wholeness, and a happiness which is grounded in a sense of bone-deep contentment. Anderson writes, "It is the intrinsic longing of the self for fulfillment which underlies the pleasure seeking instinct."[4]

And it is a fact of life, well documented in mental health practice, that we cannot live happily with others, until we can feel good about who we are. Jesus gave us this understanding when he was asked by the scribes, "What is the greatest commandment in the law?" He replied that the first and great commandment was to love God. But he tacked on another that he said was like unto the first. And that was that you should love your neighbor as you love *yourself*. It is not possible to follow that teaching and have a wholesome love of neighbor until you have a healthy sense of and appreciation for who you are.

But the journey to self fulfillment is a lonely one. It is a personal venture; no one can make it for us; we must pursue it our self. No one can grow for us. Others are a part of it and the significant people in our lives contribute to or hinder the process, but it is we alone who are the determiners of how we feel about ourselves -- our sense of self worth, our competence, our goals, and the behavior we adopt. We alone have to come to terms with who we are, our conception of what life is about, and our adjustment to the human condition.

So a part of this lonely, individual journey of growth and development is the fact of our mortality. If life is a process of becoming, there is also the reality of death which seems to be an end to an individual's growth. To have a healthy adjustment to living, we must have a healthy accommodation to the fact of our physical demise. And death is disturbing and confusing for most of us.

Most of us believe that life continues after death, over 75 percent of Americans. Yet most of us are scared out of our wits by it. Studies have shown that we shy away from the terminally ill -- friends do it, some family members do it, even doctors and nurses do it. We avoid using the word "died" and instead substitute other phrases for it like "He passed away," or "She has gone on to her reward."

So, to recap, in the growth process of life we first have the task of establishing a healthy sense of our own individuality. That development is fueled by a force that propels us continually to grow and become, to reach forward and upward. But it is a lonely enterprise for only we can grow ourselves, and we alone must accommodate to the fact of our mortality.

But the designer of life did not fashion us to be loners. People are made for relationship.

MUTUALITY

It is obvious to all of us that individuals do not exist in a vacuum. We are born into a milieu that engulfs us and of which we are a part. Yet we may not be completely cognizant of all of its characteristics or its vastness. An infant first becomes aware of mother and father, the crib, the mobile floating above, and eventually family. As the child grows, its awareness expands to neighborhood and eventually world and universe. The concept of "our world" varies from individual to individual, and as we grow and develop each of us forms a personal understanding of "what's out there" and how we fit into that.

Reality dictates the fact that we are relational beings, we are related to what we have been born into: parents, siblings, friends, neighbors, strangers, foreigners, an ecological environment, a cosmos, and a spiritual reality that we sense but do not fully understand. We interact with these "other" elements. They have an effect on who we are, what we do, how we feel, how we behave, our sexuality, our concept of the meaning and purpose of our life, our sense of well-being, our security, therefore, our ability to achieve that sense of contentment, that state of shalom that all of us seek.

Bruce C. Birch has written an insightful little book entitled *To Love As We Are Loved* that examines our human relationships and how they are modeled by God's relationship with us. His purpose was to provide a biblical grounding for understanding this relatedness "in all those aspects of human relationships that form the circumstances of our lives."[5] In it he provides insights about the freedom, vulnerability, fidelity, and wholeness that relationship affords.

In relationship we discover a freedom to become fully what we were created to be. Birch writes, "We discover that part of our full humanness which can be given only in relationship."[6] But freedom, if not balanced, can become remoteness, arrogance, aloofness. So there is a vulnerability to which relationship opens us. Relationship involves risk. Quoting

James Wharton, Birch defines vulnerability as "choosing to be so intimately involved in the story of another that what happens in their life, for good or for ill, becomes part of our own story."[7] It is through this willingness to risk that we come to really *know* each other and thereby share the experience of our humanity.

As Birch points out, if freedom and vulnerability are not tempered they can become manipulative and capricious. So therefore these characteristics of relationship must be coupled with commitment. He writes, "Relationship to another gives us the responsibility for that life to which we are related, as well as the responsibility for our own life."[8] And through healthy, loving relationship we attain that condition of wellness and wholeness, that soul-deep peace, which is characterized by the Hebrew as *shalom*. It is the attainment of this relationship to which this book addresses itself.

LIFTING OUR SIGHTS

The world in which we live is a broken place. How do we live our days so that our lives will not be broken by what surrounds us? How do we begin to make some impact on the repair of this brokenness? Well, we begin with self, for there is no other place from which to start. And even as we begin there we, at the same time, reach out to others to build healthy relationships, for we are a part of a design which is much vaster than our own person. Individuality and mutuality are tied together, we cannot have a healthy one without the other.

What ties them together? It is connection! We are relational beings. We are gregarious creatures. We long for togetherness.

Loneliness is anathema to us, it can effect us physically. We are a part of something and we crave to belong. Acceptance and a sense of belonging are primal needs of all people.

But what we belong to is not just the family of humankind that inhabits the earth. We are a part of a universe, a cosmos, a creation whose understanding confounds us. We must rise to a broader understanding of relationship, for there is a spiritual reality to our humanity and it is involved in the quality of our everyday living. Until we can know who we, as human creatures, are, where we have come from, what the purpose of our being here is -- all of which effect how we feel and act in our daily living -- we will not be able to find that shalom for which we crave.

Knowledge is power. The more we know the more we are in control because we can use that understanding to effectively order things. The more we know, the better we can understand our self and be secure about who we are, what we are a part of, what our daily living is all about, and where life can take us.

In order that we can live healthier, more fulfilled and happy lives today, in order for our daily existence to have purpose and engender a satisfaction that is deep and pervasive, we must see ourselves in the full context of that of which we are part. We must be able to see beyond the day to day and look into what transcends the here and now. Life is connected within a cosmos, a spiritual reality, and an eternity. When we can be aware of those connections we can place our self in harmony with the creation of which we are a part. Harmony promotes peace and contentment.

SOME VALUABLE VALUES

Out of the fact of our connection with these larger realities there can emerge a basic, sensible modality for living that impacts down to the level of present day affairs. There are ancient truths about relationship that have been passed down through eons of time, that have grown out of human experience with those connections. They are embodied in a certain value code that modern generations seem to have a tendency to disregard. So we thus lose this wisdom and its ability to impact our living in positive ways. An illustration of what I am referring to can be taken from the current disregard by elements in our society of what has been referred to as "family values."

In an article entitled "Guess What... God Knows Best" Glenn T. Stanton presents some scientific evidence that vindicates the Creator's idea of the family. In it he looks at pre-marital sex, the commitment of marriage, and raising children, among other things. The evidence is very revealing.

Stanton quotes a recent survey conducted by researchers at State University of New York at Stony Brook and the University of Chicago which found strong data that it is wiser to wait until marriage to engage in sexual intercourse. The study found that of all sexually active people, 'the people who reported being most physically pleased and emotionally satisfied were the married couples."[9] It goes on to say, "...physical and emotional satisfaction started to decline when people had more than one sexual partner."[10]

Married people fare better in many ways according to various studies that have been done. "Cohabiting couples compared to married couples have less healthy relationships... Marriages preceded by cohabitation are 50 to 100 percent more likely to break up than those not preceded by cohabitation... aggression is at least twice as common among cohabiters as it is among married couples... Studies on the relationship between well-being and marital status [conclude] that 'there is an intimate link between the two'... those in married relationships experience a lower rate of severe depression than people in any other category."[11]

An intact family provides the best environment in which to raise children. Stanton presents conclusions from a study by Dr. Sara McLanahan of Princeton University that reports, "Children who grow up in a household with only one biological parent are worse off, on average, than children who grow up... with both of their biological parents, regardless of the parents race or educational background."[12] The McLanahan study goes on to report, "Adolescents who have lived apart from one of their parents during some period of childhood are twice as likely to drop out of high school... to have a child before the age of 20, and one and one half times as likely to be idle -- out of school and out of work -- in their late twenties."[13]

Only when we are in position to see beyond our present worldly circumstances can we understand certain standards of conduct and the values that they imply.

Listen to some lessons from a sermon delivered by that Great Teacher Jesus and consider how our present society in general looks upon them.

> Blessed are the [humble] for theirs is the kingdom of heaven.
>
> Blessed are the meek, for they will inherit the earth.
>
> You have heard that it was said, "Eye for eye and tooth for tooth. But I tell you do not resist an evil person. If someone strikes you on the right cheek, turn to him the other also.
>
> If someone wants to take your tunic, let him have your cloak as well.
>
> You have heard that it was said, "Love your neighbor and hate your enemy. But I tell you: love your enemies and pray for those who persecute you... (Matthew 5).

Unless we have a different orientation than simply the crass world in which we live out our present days, these teachings seem not to make good sense. And only from such a position can we adopt a point of view expressed by St. Francis of Assisi in his prayer.

> Lord, make me an instrument of your peace. Where there is hatred, let me sow love, where there is injury... pardon, where there is doubt... faith, where there is despair... hope, where there is darkness... light, where there is sadness... joy.
>
> O Divine Master, grant that I may not so much seek to be consoled as to console, to be understood... as to understand, to be loved... as to love, for it is in giving that we receive, it is in pardoning, that we are pardoned, it is in dying... that we are born to eternal life. Amen.

When we come to understand and relate to all of which we are a part, we are in position to comprehend the wisdom and values that are communicated through this sense of who we are (self), where we have come from, what we are a part of (which includes others), and where life is designed to go. We will find that this has a tremendous impact on how we feel and what we do in the present.

In beginning the journey to understand these connections, we must more fully comprehend the seriousness of our separation. Therefore, the next chapter will begin with a case study which will depict the awful trauma that can eventuate from our disconnection and alienation. It will do this through the medium of what looks like, from the outside, an All-American family.

CHAPTER 2:
AND WE'RE ALIENATED

She entered my office that first day with a shallow smile on her lips, but her sad eyes harbored a quiet inner despair. Betsy was a young woman whom I judged to be in her early twenties. In that first moment of meeting I could see what her face reflected, but I could not yet know what was in her heart.

"Why are you here?" I asked. And with that question we embarked on an intimate journey together which would extend over a period of many months. It would be a journey on which Betsy would slowly open to me that heart which harbored the anguish I saw in her eyes.

Through the relationship which evolved from our first meeting, I was witness again to the destructive force of a brokenness that infects our human relationships and an alienation that attests to our separation from that of which we are a natural part.

In what follows in this book, I will share with you what I saw in the lives of people who shared the deepest parts of themselves with me. In the telling, I will disguise all persons to protect confidentiality, but the substance of the accounts will be absolutely authentic.

INSIDE A DEPRESSION

What began to spill out was like raw sewage that had spoiled inside Betsy for a very long time. She had no place to dump it; no one cared enough to want to listen. It came out filtered through a depression that was apparent in her appearance, in her posture, in the way she spoke, and in what she said.

"I'm here," she replied, in response to my original question, "because I need help in figuring out why I feel this way."

"How do you feel?" I asked. "I feel lost, confused, angry all the time. I feel alone and helpless. My life is a complete failure. I don't like the person I've become."

If you saw Betsy on the street, in the hospital where she works as a licensed practical nurse, in the register line at the food market, you would never suspect any of these feelings of isolation and worthlessness. She and her three year old daughter were living with her parents and sister because she was separated from her husband. They had no idea of Betsy's inner torment. Although Betsy wanted to be a good daughter and a loving sister, these intentions were often undercut by her hot temper which would flare up with great frequency.

Her husband had no idea what Betsy was feeling deep inside that sanctum of "self" where she hid from sight that which she felt unsafe in sharing. "I only knew him six months when we were married. I was pregnant. I didn't love him, but I did want it to work. I tried to be superwife and supermom. I went to work, cleaned, cooked, cared for my daughter. But we fought. Mostly because he wouldn't work and because he took money I earned to buy drugs. After two years I left.

"We were separated for a year and then I went back. He seemed to have changed, but I found he really hadn't. He was always putting me down. So I left again. I suppose I should have put up with more, maybe then it would have worked."

Betsy has a wry grin which goes along with a kind of devilishness in some of her facial expressions that is a part of her sense of humor. She uses that sense of humor to mask what she is really feeling.

And wrestling with those feelings, which are bottled up inside of herself, consumes so much emotional energy that she has no vitality left for much else. She is too drained for any kind of social activity. She does not want to get up in the morning. She feels sleepy all the time. She doesn't want to go to work, or to a movie, or shopping at the mall.

There is nothing coming into Betsy's life to feed and renew her psychic energy, no emotional warmth directed at her. She has no feeling of belonging, therefore no sense of value or worthiness. No one is there to hold her, comfort her, hug and kiss her. No one to make the many other little gestures of intimate togetherness, that tell her she is important and that she is loved.

She compensates by taking in food; she goes on eating binges. Betsy is overweight, but that gives her a body image which she feels matches her general feeling about herself. "I'm not a very attractive person," she says.

THE UNCONNECTED FAMILY

The key to understanding Betsy's feelings of worthlessness, but still her great hunger for the acceptance and affection which is a basic need of our humanity, lies in her childhood. What John Milton wrote is so true, "The childhood shows the man, as morning shows the day."

"My parents loved us," she told me, "they tried to give us all the toys and clothes and advantages that all the other kids had. We had a good home; mom and dad both worked hard. At Christmas and for our birthdays there were always lots of gifts."

As Betsy went on, she pictured growing up in a home that by all outward appearances would be classified as a good, middle-class family situation. Their house was in a neighborhood of other families that were similar to theirs. Father worked in a blue collar job; and, although mother also worked, she still became involved with the school PTA and took an interest in community affairs.

The parents provided opportunities that would enhance the education and skills of their two daughters -- dance and music lessons, sports activities. In all, Betsy pictured what we might think of as the typical American family. But the typical family is a myth, an illusion that does not exist in reality. For inside the walls of our homes and the skins of our own personhood, we are all unique.

What was it about this supposedly "typical" environment in which Betsy grew up that produced her depression and sense of worthlessness? Where did her deep feeling of aloneness come from, growing up in the bosom of such a family group? Why did she see herself as a "failure" and "not a good person?" Why did she feel detached, alone, afraid, unsure of herself, hesitant to act on her own feelings and ideas? Why doesn't she like herself? From whence did that deep anger generate that comes out as a nasty temper?

The answers to these questions have their roots in the years of infancy and childhood. Our perceptions begin in the earliest moments of our living. We know today that even in the womb new life is developing important sensitivities, awareness and responses.

Early in her life Betsy was experiencing her parent's attitudes, behaviors, values, and priorities, all of which would significantly mold, shape, and condition the person whom she would become. The manner in which she was fed, held, and treated; the way she was attended to when she cried; how she was put to bed; how she was responded to when she had a problem or need; how her feelings were treated when she expressed them; these and the thousands of ways that parents and child interact convey to the child important messages about his/her value as an individual.

Betsy says, referring to her mother, "I'm not sure she loves me."

"Why not," I asked.

Then she goes on, "I don't think she really cares about me. She ignores me, keeps things to herself. She never shows any emotion. She always wanted to put on this great front as a family. 'Family is everything,' she used to tell us. She had this idea about what she wanted us to be like. All the things they provided for us, the dance lessons, the music lessons, the sports, were really so that we could achieve this appearance that she wanted us to have.

"She never asked what I wanted. She never took it seriously when I would tell her what I wanted. She and dad would get very angry when I did not do what they wanted me to do. When I would do something they wanted so that they would be pleased I would get candy or a toy, but never a hug. The only time mom hugged me was when I would cry."

There were tears rolling down her cheeks as she finished. I felt her emptiness and pain.

Betsy thought her dad was "the best man I know." She describes him as sensitive and caring, but a "worrier." "I would go to dad when I was hurt," she says, "but I did not go often." Despite these feelings, however, there was not the warmth and supportive relationship here that would be expected from such remarks.

"I was afraid to talk to him," she says. "We were always afraid we would upset him, because when he was upset he would get mad. When he was mad he would make me feel bad. I could never tell him how I felt, I was afraid he would 'put me down,' like, 'Oh grow up, Betsy, don't be such a baby.' My dad still makes me feel incompetent because I don't do things the way he thinks I should. He tries to control me. He only hugs me when he wants something."

I asked Betsy about the relationship between her mother and father. She told me, "Mom gives daddy nothing. She is as closed with him as with the rest of us. She comes home from work late at night and dad makes insinuating remarks about "out playing around."

He wants her companionship and when he doesn't get it he is angry and picks at her. They do not have a happy marriage. I don't really think they love each other. I expect them to get a divorce some day."

What emerges from Betsy's statements is the picture of a mother, father, and daughter who are separated, not able to share with one another, living together as family but operating in emotional detachment. There is no feeling of "oneness," or "wholeness" between them. Rather than being together in a supportive and mutually enhancing relationship in which each is invested in the other, they are isolated and in conflict. In such an environment Betsy was unable to receive the affirmation and love that all people need as children in order to become healthy, self-actualizing, and happy persons.

THE UNCONNECTED CHILD

When things do not go well in a young child's life, when they do not receive the affection all children need and crave, when there is discord in their home, they blame themselves. They cannot blame their parents, for to a young child adults are like gods. They are all-knowing, they are all-powerful, and they are in control.

So the psychology of the child works against his/herself and says, "It has to be my fault. I must be bad; I must not be acceptable; I must not be lovable; if I were better, it wouldn't be this way." And with this kind of immature reasoning children take on false conceptions of self which they carry with them for the rest of their lives, lives that are a distorted caricature of what they might have been.

Gary Smalley and John Trent have written an entire book that deals with the need we all have to receive the loving affirmation of our parents. Their title is *The Blessing*[1] and it is this need for the confirmation and approval of our parents that is their focus. These authors make a very convincing case for the fact that without this "blessing", children can become a disfigured distortion of what they have the potential to become.

Under such circumstances children, the authors point out, can become "seekers," always searching for an intimacy which, when they get close to it, they can hardly tolerate. They can be "shattered," living deeply troubled lives over the loss of their parents' love and acceptance. Or they may become "smotherers," so emotionally empty that they steamroller spouses, children, friends, and workmates with their unmet needs and drain these others of their capacity to listen or help.

Children can become "the angry," carrying animosity over their loss for the rest of their lives, distracted from intimacy in other relationships.

"The detached" are those who spend a lifetime protecting themselves from the same thing happening to them again. Trying to earn the approval they never received is the tactic of "the driven," who are the perfectionists, the workaholics, and the notorious overachievers. And finally there are "the seduced," who look for the never received love in all the wrong places. They become the promiscuous, the compulsive gamblers, the alcoholics, and the drug abusers. Betsy became one of "the seduced."

GOOD PEOPLE CAN DO BAD THINGS

Humanity is designed for relationship. We are born equipped in every way, physically, mentally, and psychologically, for that potential. But if corrupted by our early development or our own mindset, what was given to us at birth will be distorted.

Betsy's parents were not bad people; there was no streak of meanness in them. If you asked, they would tell you that they loved their two daughters and they really believed that; look at what they had provided for them. Family, they both said, was important and they were working hard to provide what was necessary to build that "all American" image.

They wanted to be happy, earn respect and feel secure. But they weren't achieving that perfectness that they sought. "Why not?" they must have wondered. What was going wrong? They were in no position to understand it, but their tactics were flawed. The way that we parent our children is the product of the parenting we received and the environment in which we grew up. This is the only model we have.

Betsy's mother grew up in a very dysfunctional family. Her father left when she was very young and she never knew him. He completely disappeared from their lives and never contacted them or sent any support. Her mother worked hard to make ends meet and there wasn't much time or energy left to spend with the children. Her mother would marry again, twice, but each marriage would end in divorce after a rather unhappy relationship.

As a result, Betsy's mother would grow into an adult who never learned how to be close and intimate. In fact, she probably feared closeness, because she did not want a repeat of that awful feeling of getting close and then being deserted. Yet she needed affection and the sense of personal worth and security that comes from intimacy, as we all do. So Betsy's mom sought her value as a person and her security in hard work, keeping her distance emotionally, and trying to create the family that was so important to her, the family she never really had.

So Betsy, her child, became a "piece" in the mother's dream of happiness and security. There was a certain place for Betsy in that ideal and mother pushed and pressured to assure that her daughter would fill that slot. And her mother would see no error in that. After all, wasn't the goal for everyone to be together in this perfect union which she was working so hard to create? The problem, of course, a problem her mother could not see from her perspective, was that Betsy's personhood and her need for affection and validation were lost in her mother's personal quest.

Betsy's father was a perfect conscript in her mother's efforts to build that which was so important for her. Both parents were united in creating that family image that they wanted to portray. It was an image they needed for their own sense of security and well-being, and for the rest of the world to see and admire. So father joined in the campaign to shape the children in the mold of that image.

His model for parenting was his quiet, but stern autocratic father, a father who demanded strict compliance to his requirements for his children. It was a model in which the show of affection was not part of manliness. There was a sensitivity for compassion and fellow-feeling in Betsy's father, however, which he received from his loving and understanding mother. But he allowed that warmth to show only in infrequent moments. This was the side of him that Betsy saw as "the best man I know."

So the parenting Betsy experienced from her father mirrored that which she received from her mother. Be this kind of a child, grow into this kind of person that we need you to be. We will provide what is necessary to support you in your development. And these "things," what you will become, and what you will be a part of will be your rewards. Approval did not come through the show of affection and the overt expression of love, behavior which the growing-up conditions of both parents did not prepare them to give. Approval came in the form of toys and candy and "things" when Betsy would fulfill her parent's image of what they wanted her to be.

Where then did this set of life circumstances leave Betsy? She tells us with her own words. "Nobody loves me," she says as the tears again well up in her eyes. "I feel like a damn burden that keeps my mother from getting what she wants. I don't feel like I have a family; I feel alone. I'm not important to anyone, they never talk to me, confide in me. I never know what's going on. There is always conflict between us and I know I'm a part of it, but I don't want to be. I want them to love me. I don't want to be alone. But I can't tell them. I'm afraid to tell them. This is the only place that I can cry."

And in one last, desperate sentence Betsy shares with me the real thorn that lies deep in that wounded heart, making it bleed with an awful, sad, aloneness, "I just want to feel like I'm wanted."

TOGETHER BUT APART

"I want to belong!" was Betsy's desperate necessity. She needed to feel connected. But her need went deeper than just physical proximity, it was an innate hunger of her soul, of her humanity. This crying out to be "a part of" was a condition of her psyche, her inner person. Betsy needed to be wanted in the way that love craves to unite with its beloved.

"I want to belong," was also the desperate cry of each of her parents. They too had the same need embedded in the core of what they were. It evidenced itself in their drive to become the "All American" family. "Family is important," they preached to their children. Mother and father each needed to "connect" with others in the way that love bonds individuals in soul satisfying relationship. They just didn't know how to make the connections.

Connection is the very substance of human life. It is a reality of the human psyche that we need to feel joined with one another. We need to be a part of some reality that gives us a sense of belonging, identity, value, meaning, and purpose.

But we don't have to be told that, for deep inside every person there is an innate hunger for attachment. We reach out for connection; we live in families; we develop friendships; we marry; we organize ourselves in social groups, in communities, in nations. We join together to build. We huddle together when afraid. We seek company to enjoy our recreations. We live bound together in relationships; association is the fabric of life. The loneliness of separation is anathema to us.

Yet look at the character that our togetherness often takes on. In Betsy's family we observed alienation among individuals who, in the core of their selfhood, had the same necessity to be loved. We saw that there was no harmonic relationship between the individuals who thought of themselves as "family," yet were unable to come together with any unity of purpose and mutual well-being.

Their condition of detachment occurred because in their search for the solace that a loving relationship yields, they had not learned how to love. They were so focused on what they wanted and were striving to construct to fulfill themselves, that they could not see the needs of the others. Such a self-centered preoccupation dooms the possibility of loving relationship, for love is an investment of "self" in "other."

As loving as they appeared to be in the provisions that they made for their children, the case review showed mother and father focused on their own agendas. Ultimately, this was the cause of Betsy's alienation as she felt used rather than loved.

This case review provokes even broader questions, "Are modern people able to connect with each other heart to heart, at some core level of our humanity that bonds us in a spirit of oneness and wholeness? Does our being together yield a sense of comradeship, commonality, security, contentment, and joy? Does our connection lead us to that beautiful state of being which the Hebrews call shalom? Or do we, in our togetherness, remain at some fundamental level, separate and apart, divided by an individuality that blocks our meeting spirit to spirit, each related to the other in a universality that goes beyond the mere satisfaction of our own personal needs and appetites?

Thomas Wolfe perceived a separateness that exists in our togetherness. In his life he felt a separateness that extends across our humanity and defines a condition of isolation among us. He wrote, "The whole conviction of my life now rests on the belief that loneliness, far from being some curious rare phenomenon peculiar to myself and a few other solitary souls, in fact, is the central, inevitable fact of human existence."[2]

Are we all, like Betsy, unconnected strangers searching for that sense of wholeness and well-being? Have we gotten lost because of our self-willed alienation from the Creator's eternal system? Do we have to be strangers to God and each other, and be alone? Across the ages there have been those who say this is a violation of the natural condition. There are those who have been pointing out a fundamental, underlying connectedness between all things, a connectedness between persons, other living things, and even inanimate matter. It is a "fitting together" according to some unseen fabric that underlies the entire cosmos.

This is a conception identified with Mysticism, a position that has often been maligned and misunderstood, but deserves a more serious consideration. Scott Peck in his book *The Different Drum* writes, "...they (the Mystics) are the ones most aware that the whole world is a community and realize that what divides us into warring camps is precisely the lack of this awareness. Having become practiced at emptying themselves of preconceived notions and prejudices and able to perceive the invisible underlying fabric that connects everything, they do not think in terms of factions or blocs or even national boundaries; they know this to be one world."[3]

"Love" and "alienation" are opposite conditions of relationship that mark off two extremities. Love is what connects us. It brings us together and maintains harmonic relationship. In the absence of love we are separated; we are isolated, and therefore in conflict. That is alienation. What Betsy sought and was unable to find was that sense of peace which comes from knowing that you are a valued part of something, that you are wanted and loved. What all people want is the same sense of well-being that comes from peaceful coexistence.

STRANGERS IN A LONELY CROWD

There is a larger tragedy brought to light in the review of this family's interpersonal relationships. For the situation we see in this small group is a microcosm of what we find if we honestly look at our human condition in general: in our world family we observe the syndrome of alienation. As people who share a common humanity we are not connected by that commonality. There is a separation that divides us preventing the achievement of any unity in purpose and well-being.

We do not live in harmony with each other nor with the cosmic system of which we are a part. We live as isolated entities attempting to satisfy the deep needs of our soul for survival, attachment, attention, acceptance, nurturing, peace, happiness, and love. We have failed to see that this detachment is the very cause of our failure to find that inner personal peace and contentment which can exist only as we are together in community. We are estranged from each other and that of which we are a natural part. We have become strangers, living together but "detached from" and therefore lonely -- strangers in a lonely crowd.

Our condition has been observed by Paul Tillich who brings its reality right down to the personal level as he writes,

> Who has not at some time, been lonely in the midst of a social event? The feeling of our separation from the rest of life is most acute when we are surrounded by it in noise and talk. We realize then much more than in moments of solitude how strange we are to each other, how estranged life is from life... The walls of distance, in time and space, have been removed by technical progress; but the

> walls of estrangement between heart and heart
> have been incredibly strengthened.[4]

It is not hard to make this case for the state of alienation among us. All we need do is look at the record of discord that has existed and continues to exist in our world: the intrigue between nations, war, terrorism, religious intolerance, apartheid, animosity between ethnic groups, Hitler's "final solution," the "ethnic cleansing" in the former state of Yugoslavia, Neo-Nazism, the disparity between the "have" and the "have not" countries, and the list goes on.

But lest we look at these generalities, that may be distant from some of our lives and therefore easy to admit but also dismiss, let us turn our focus closer to home. James Patterson and Peter Kim have done an in-depth scientific study in which they took the moral pulse of Americans in the 1990's. They used state-of-the-art research techniques that go much beyond trivial personal interviews to probe the ethics, values, and beliefs of our time.

Their book *The Day America Told the Truth* reports their findings. They write, "The United States has become greedier, meaner, colder, more selfish, and a more uncaring place. This is no wild inferential speculation but, rather, the informed consensus of the American people."[5] They document the violence we perpetrate against each other and observe that our country "is far and away the most violent industrialized nation on the earth."[6] We are strangers to our closest neighbors, for as the study found "The great majority of Americans (72 percent) openly admit that they don't know the people next door."[7]

The anecdotal record of these findings occur in the news reports we read: fraud; embezzlement; murder; date-rape; child, spouse and elderly parent abuse in families; the divorce rate; the "wilding" of teenage gangs; the unconcern of bystanders who "don't want to get involved;" and again, the list goes on.

And this alienation is not just an estrangement from each other; it is a detachment from the very system that supports our existence. In disregard of ecological realities we "foul our own nest." We build our homes and factories without regard to the balancing of all life in the environment. We trample delicate life systems with our off-road vehicles and the contaminants that destroy the ozone of our atmosphere and the coral reefs in the seas. We litter, crush, and destroy without regard to what has taken eons of time to build, that which services our own life support. In his book *Creation For What?* Paul Huber notes,

> Indeed a great many scientists, sociologists, and theologians are alarmed and distressed by the growing propensity in all segments of society for "doing what's good for me first," which is pointing humanity toward the path of self-destruction. They see that people have generally exploited their environment and have exploited each other, in every case in order to satisfy their own immediate, selfish objectives, to the degree that society is now faced with multitudinous, critical, world problems.[8]

We are alienated.

THE FABRIC OF LIFE

The very fabric of our lives is connection. Connection with another, connection with some reality that gives us a sense of belonging, identity, value, meaning, and purpose. Perhaps, then, the basic personal problem we face is that we have lost connection with that which identifies who we are, who we belong with, what the meaning and purpose of life is, and where life is ultimately going, all of which are the ingredients of an ultimate sense of value.

If we are alienated from each other and from our environment, perhaps it is because we are alienated from the Creator of the system and the mechanics of that system. Thus, through eons of separation, we may have forgotten who we are and from whence we came. Thus, as individuals, we are personally lost in a confusion that has erased from our memory the eternal design of which human life is the keystone and the purpose we serve, and that serves us, in that design.

Thus we are bored with the mandated routines in our life. Thus there is an emptiness within us that we seek to fill with pleasures that do not bring lasting happiness. Thus the global family into which life was born has become dismembered and now we flounder about, knocking together in discord, afraid to face our own mortality, and seeking to create for ourselves that which our inner heart craves as an ancient memory of what existed in a far-off past. In response to these suppositions, consider the hypothesis below.

Connection with the Creator of this system of which we are a part is the very substance of our humanity, what it means to be human. Yet in the earliest moments of our history women and men, using the power of choice (free will), which is a mark of our humanity, turned away from an early bond with the

Creator of life to set themselves up as independent entities in control of their own well-being and destiny.

This renunciation meant also that humanity would lose touch with a part of itself, a part that knows its place in the design of things, a part that can admit its own finiteness and vulnerability, a part that can experience dependency. Therefore we've lost a part that can be open to that which can bring us to the fullness of our potential for connection: loving relationship with God and with each other.

And because the original connection was with the only source of true love (that Creating Power whose love provided life and thus defined loving relationship), it is only through that Source and harmony with the eternal system It created that that lost part can be re-experienced at all.

But that, unfortunately, becomes the ultimate paradox. For while humanity hungers to recapture the renounced part of itself, so as to enjoy that experience of shalom, it also remains forever careful about any relationship with an "Other" whose intimacy and intensity are strong enough to recall that archaic bond within which shalom was first experienced. Thus humanity keeps itself rigidly separate, tightly under control so as not to lose the fabricated illusion of its own power and independence.

This is an important clue, then, in understanding that void in our own life and why human relationships with each other are, on the whole, self-centered and emotionally unfulfilled. The heart and intensity of people's need is to connect with the Source of their humanity. And this, too, is why human beings often appear dependent and unfulfilled while at the same time denying it so insistently. It is the reason why we believe in the continuation of life, but are not really sure of it. It is why we cannot see beyond physical death to the reality of eternal life with any conviction that defuses our fear. The root of the denial is the unconscious need to maintain the fabricated illusion of the Great Lie: we are the gods of our own lives.

And so we hang in the grip of a powerful combination of need and fear, a need for a personal peace within ourselves and in our world, coupled with the fear of loss of control of our own lives -- which we don't seem to realize we can't completely control anyhow. In that dilemma we have lost an important part of our self.

THE LOSS OF SELF

Would you believe that people can lose a part of themselves? Would you believe they can lose a part of who they are, a part of the inner "me" by which we identify ourselves? It is true, this can and does happen. And it happens to a degree that you might not suspect. Listen to a case that illustrates the point. If you looked at Wilma she would appear to be "intact." If you spoke to Wilma you would find her able to interact socially with you in an acceptable manner. Nothing that you would perceive would indicate that she was anything but a healthy, well-adjusted person. But Wilma is not whole. She is not emotionally healthy. She is not a well-adjusted person.

An important segment of Wilma's personhood has been lost and this prevents her from achieving an inner comfortableness about herself. She lives in a state of anxiety, off balance, always trying to "read" other people and properly "fit in" so as to be accepted. She is never sure of herself, questions whether she has done the right thing, struggles in indecision about the most routine kinds of choices. She lacks confidence in herself to do anything appropriately. Wilma lives as if she is walking in a world covered with egg shells, tip-toeing about, trying desperately not to offend so that she will be acceptable.

If you got to know her more intimately, you would pick up on her problem. You would sense that Wilma struggles in living. What is wrong?

Wilma has lost a part of herself. It is not a physical part, but an element of her inner person. She has lost touch with her feelings. We are our feelings; our feelings are us. When the validity of our inner experience -- how we process what happens to us, how we react to that, how we desire to move and grow, what we want and what we feel -- is not legitimized and is thereby taken from us, then we have lost a part of what we are.

When this happens, our personal integrity is violated and we are incapacitated in the same way we would be physically handicapped by the loss of sight or limb. In such a condition we are not equipped to fully function. The person who we are is damaged and the person we could be never emerges. We lose the opportunity to become who we really could be.

THE LOSS OF SOUL

In a certain respect, a great many people in the world are like Wilma, they have lost touch with a part of themselves. But it is a different part of us that many of us have lost. Like Wilma's feelings, it is a part that we cannot find when we look at our self in the mirror, but it is as real as what we do see in the reflection. In fact, it is the living essence that empowers the body. It has been likened to the hand that is inside the glove -- without the hand the glove is lifeless.

What we are talking about here is what we commonly refer to as the soul. It is the spiritual aspect of our humanity which is capable of perceiving and interacting with the realm that lies outside the physical. We have lost touch with that aspect of our humanity simply out of neglect. We've ignored it. But although many people have chosen not to countenance it, that part of us has not disappeared. Its reality and the benefits of that reality are still a functional part of what we are.

Restoring the soul's vitality to our living is simply a matter of giving it cognizance.

It is easy to dismiss or ignore what is not visible. The physical is obvious to us. It is the world in which we live. It is the things of earth and sky and sea. It is our body through which we experience the world and have our being.

But that other part of us that does not show up in the mirror, is the "me" that lives inside the body. The hand in the glove. It is the part of us that is our real self. This part incorporates the body in its image, because we cannot conceive ourselves without our physical parts. But we know that the torso, the arms, the legs, the fingers, and the toes are not "us." They are not the living essence that uses these parts to operate in our environment. The body alone is not "us."

The real "us" is that "life" that projects itself into the world from out of the mind. As we noted in an earlier chapter, St. Augustine teaches that the soul is the "terminus where the life propelling power is joined with the physical body.

And there is a place in the right temporal lobe of the brain, within the Sylvian fissure, which research leads some scientists to identify as the genetic mechanism that enables us to perceive the things of God. This area, of which we shall present more later, explains the reality of a mechanism in our body that is attuned with and able to connect with a province outside the physical realm. It is a realm in which natural law does not apply, therefore, a place we cannot fully fathom. But we know it exists because, as we shall see, we have revelation, personal experience, and some data coming as a result of scientific research, that attests to the fact of "something out there."

Now we will turn to look at the realities of this link between our "us" and what it is that's "out there" and in the process perceive things about the connection with our daily living. We will take that tour as we examine our cosmic connection, our Divine connection, and our eternal connection.

PART II: BUT WE'RE CONNECTED TO A COSMOS

Every part of this earth is sacred.
Every shining pine needle, every sandy shore, every mist in the dark woods,
every clearing and humming insect is holy.
The rocky crest, the juices of the meadow,
the beasts and the people,
all belong to the same family.
Teach your children the earth is our mother.
Whatever befalls the earth, befalls the children of the earth.
The water's murmur is the voice of our father's father,
we are part of the earth, and the earth is part of us.
The rivers are our brothers; they quench our thirst.
The perfumed flowers are our sisters.
The air is precious, for all of us share the same breath.
The wind that gave our grandparents breath also receives their last sign.
The wind gave our children the spirit of life.
This we know, the earth does not belong to us; we belong to the earth.
This we know, all things are connected.
Our God is the same God, whose compassion is equal to all.
For we did not weave the web of life; we are merely a strand in it.
   Whatever we do to the web, we do to ourselves.
   Let us give thanks for the web and the circle that connects us.
   Thanks be to God, the God of all.
Chief Seattle

Yearning For Eden/

CHAPTER 3:
NATURE'S DANCE

Charles Dickens in his book Martin Chuzzlewit has his main character explain to his cohort Pecksniff the importance of their affiliation. Chuzzlewit says to his associate, "We are the two halves of a pair of scissors, when apart, Pecksniff, but together we are something." The importance of being together, feeling connected cannot be underestimated. Consider the following cases.

CONNECTION AND FEELING GOOD

Chuck was the owner of his own small business. He had come to see me because, he had said, "I feel like I'm in pieces, my whole world is coming apart. I'm not sleeping well, I can't concentrate, I'm irritable with my employees, I feel weighted down, I'm on edge all the time."

Yearning For Eden/

Chuck's wife had left him temporarily and was caring for her ill mother in another state. But she had gone to her mother's also because she had told Chuck, "I need to get away from you." Their relationship had been abrasive lately and his wife frankly admitted she was testing the possibility of divorce. He missed her and felt abandoned and lonely.

The business was not doing well, either. Income was being drained by an unprofitable satellite office, a key employee had quit, and, in his wife's absence, Chuck had to take over her responsibilities for the accounting operation. It was no wonder that he was depressed, stressed out, angry, anxious, and lonely. Literally, Chuck's world was coming apart.

There is a feeling of togetherness that is necessary to our sense of security and well-being. When the elements that compose "our world" drift out of orb, there is an anxiousness that overtakes us. It is a survival anxiety. Are we going to be able to make it?

This survival anxiety, I believe, is the root of our restless quest for Eden, the hunger that goes unquenched by the things of our material world, the "getting" and "having." Because we have lost touch with the spiritual elements of our humanity, there is an inner sense of incompleteness. We feel it, but many have not fathomed its etiology. When we are able to do that and reestablish the connection that we have lost, then we can experience that fulfillment that leads to the shalom for which we search.

And it is possible to do that. Scott Peck documents such a dramatic turnabout from one of his cases with a patient he calls Marcia.[1] This woman in her mid-twenties had come to Dr. Peck troubled by a generalized anhedonia, a state of inexplicable joylessness. She was raised in a well-to-do home by parents who were atheists. She too declared herself to be "a true atheist" when she began her therapy.

Her treatment centered about her parents who, while providing for her economically, were distant and withdrawn from her emotionally. Peck describes her as "the proverbial 'poor little rich girl,' a psychological orphan." The key element in her improvement was the relationship she developed with her therapist, which contrasted sharply from the relationship she had had with her parents. Experiencing this different way of "connecting," Marcia began to come out of her joyless state.

Her change of attitude was reflected in her own statement. "Even though I'm still here, living in the same old house and doing some of the same old things, the whole world looks very different, feels very different. It feels warm and safe and loving and exciting and good. I remember telling you I was an atheist. I'm not sure I am any more. In fact, I don't think I am."

Yearning For Eden/

And then she goes on to make this statement that reflects the extraordinary meaning the sense of being "connected" has on our everyday functioning. "Its funny. I don't know how to talk about this sort of thing. I just feel connected, real, like I'm a real part of a very big picture, and even though I can't see much of the picture, I know its there and I know its good and I know I'm a part of it."

Marcia was experiencing the first moments of her discovery of "heaven" while still being on earth!

A SYMBIOTIC SYSTEM

To extend our knowledge and understand more about important issues of living, the scientist constantly uses his microscope to look into the teeming life that goes on out of sight of the naked eye. In the same way, we can learn from that life that abounds around us, not out of our sight, but tucked away in its own nitch, assiduously doing its own thing hour by hour, out of the immediate concern of our conscious awareness. We can glimpse insights in the micro world that can open for us truths about the macro, the larger system of which human life is one part.

Science is teaching us today that as we learn more and more about this vast cosmic picture, the abyss between the macrocosm and the microcosm, the very big and the very little,

Yearning For Eden/

is being bridged and the whole complex of the universe is resolving into a homogeneous fabric. In this chapter we will examine that fabric in light of the teaching of present knowledge, but also, in the next, we will weave into our inspection the wisdom of ancient experience.

So let us begin with the ant, that lowly insect that every young child at one time or another has bent over to watch, observing in fascinated discovery the frantic activity of the "hill," or the industrious gathering chores of the "workers." Social life among Hymenoptera attains its highest level in ants.

As we observe their colonies, a complex organization of relationships becomes apparent. There can be a million of these insects connected in community, each one ceaselessly and compulsively working to add perfection to his area of their life enterprise. And each ant does this without the faintest notion of what is going on elsewhere. Workers, soldiers, queens each live out their life in a social establishment that has been going on through eons of time.

Generations may vanish in a month or so, yet the hill can go on, given favorable conditions, forever. Each individual comes into that community to perform its work with infallible, undistracted skill amidst the confusion of the general enterprise. The whole colony is contributing to the right configurations for

Yearning For Eden/

the warmth and ventilation of the eggs and larvae, and the preservation of the life cycle.

Now this is not to infer that this programmed behavior of ants in any way can serve as a mechanical model for human social organization; it absolutely cannot. There are elements in our humanity that are completely distinctive and unique that would make any such inference ridiculous. These elements make us what we are and make us vastly different from all other forms of life.

But as we observe the life pattern of the anthill, what we notice is a connectional system that works together, in harmony, for the promotion of life, both of the individual organism and the colony in general. There is apparent an invisible schema, invisible to the eye but detected in the unified motive of the hill's occupants, that guides and directs the unfolding life of each ant and the destiny of the its colony. This is genetically based, instinctive behavior, to be sure, yet the deeper reality is that there lies behind such behavior some relational system within which instinct has developed and of which instinct serves the purpose.

As each living unit in the colony relates in synchrony with each other and with the operational mode of that system, individual and community life in the anthill continues generation after generation. Together they successfully maintain the

Yearning For Eden/

continued existence of the colony. In the social organization of the ant, we see a relational system whose healthy function promotes life.

If we raise our eyes from the ground and look upward to the extremities of telescopic sight and knowledge we also see elements of the universe existing in relationship. The planets of our solar system, with their various moons, move in patterned relationship, so precise that they can be defined with mathematical exactitude. If we peer into the electron microscope it opens the world of the atom, each defined by relationships of protons and neutrons that can be described by algebraic formula and whose behavior can be predicted by such formulas. Our own bodies function as a biological system whose health is a statement of the balanced, interactive connection of literally billions of individual elements.

As with the genetic behavior of the ant, behind all this connectedness there is apparent an invisible weave of fabric, detectable in the coordination of each system, whose composition acts to form together its constituent elements in harmonic relationship. And in this way life moves on.

Nature is a seemingly endless amalgam of patterned relationships, the extent of which we are still discovering. It was the development of the computer and its calculating powers that

Yearning For Eden/

has brought into view systems that before this technology's time lay outside the normal human scale of things.

By writing mathematical formulas that describe the dynamic forces operating in nature, then feeding these numerical descriptions into the computer, it is possible to view on a monitor's screen the designs that before have not been visible to us. These formulas act to direct the computer's output on the screen in the same way that DNA chromosomes act to direct the development of life forms in nature.

It is not the purpose here to detail the technicalities of this newest system of what is called "fractal geometry," developed by Benoit Mendelbrodt of Harvard University. Nor does this writer have the credentials to do so. What we do want to do, however, is note some of the documented knowledge about nature's system that we have derived from this new method of looking at things. In describing the dynamics of nature, fractals and the computer have provided some most dramatic revelations.

ORDER IN DISORDER

"Fractal images" describe the complexities in nature by reducing these complexities, on a smaller and smaller scale, thus helping us to reduce the complex to simple, comprehensible units. For example, the branching process of

Yearning For Eden/

an oak tree, which in its entirety is an intricate and complicated labyrinth, can be diminished to a single geometric shape, repeated over and over on many different scales. The DNA of the tree guides the construction of the mighty oak by repeating a simple branching pattern over and over, from the massive trunk to the finest veins of a leaf.

It is as if we looked at a huge design of small, connected lines on a very large poster, but were able to trace the pattern down to a simple equilateral triangle on which other equilateral triangles were repeated over and over on each side of each triangle. By being able to see into nature's processes in this way, we have discovered that nature's structures are a system of simple elements, repeated again and again in connected relationship on many different scales, from small to large -- micro to macro.

By using fractal geometry as an investigative tool it has been found that this ordered process of nature exists even in what we have known as disorder. In other words, even in chaos we are discovering order -- the spontaneous appearance of patterns in apparent randomness.

Scientists at the University of Texas asked if there were a structure concealed in the turbulence of a flowing stream as there is a genetic pattern within a flower. And is there a geometric order in the crest of a wave? When they investigated

Yearning For Eden/

these possibilities using this new tool, they found a surprising regular behavior emerges.

For example they found, as a wave approached total turbulence, finer and finer structures appeared within the body of the wave. And these changes repeated themselves each time the experiment was carried out. There is order in turbulence! There is patterned relationship even in what we see as disorder!

We also know that in nature these individual systems -- like the anthill, the planetary complex, atoms, animal organisms of all types, trees, and so on -- link together in larger functional units. Thus we have the solar system which is a part of its galaxy. We have ecological regions in which life for all elements in the region is maintained and promoted by a delicate balance between its individual units.

Lewis Thomas in his book *The Lives of a Cell* describes a protozoan organism, Myxotricha paradoxa, that is a combination of individual life forms.

> His celia are not cilia at all, but individual spirochetes, and at the base of attachment of each spirochete is an oval organella, embedded in the myxotricha membrane, which is a bacterium. It is not an animal after all -- it is a company, an assemblage.[2]

Thomas goes on to point out, "There is a tendency for living things to join up, establish linkages, live inside each other,

Yearning For Eden/

return to earlier arrangements, get along, whenever possible. This is the way of the world."[3]

Thomas observes this tendency and concludes, "There is an underlying force that drives together the several creatures comprising the myxotricha, and then drives the assemblage into union with the termite. ...It might turn out that the same tendency underlies the joining together of organisms into communities, communities into ecosystems, and ecosystems into the biosphere."[4]

What we perceive from these understandings is that if we were able to go out far enough, detach ourselves and fly out beyond this cosmic system of which we are part, that we would look in on it and see a huge, complicated labyrinth formed as a single unit, composed of uncountable fields of energies, designed to function together in harmonic relationship for the promotion of its life. If we could put it all together in one gigantic design, would we not see what science is pointing us toward: that there is no abyss between the macrocosm and the microcosm, the very big and the very little, the whole complex of the universe is one homogeneous fabric?

At the heart of nature is there not a simple life process, repeated over and over, again and again, on many different scales, small and large, like the branching of the oak tree, which is attuned to a grand purpose for it all? Can that not be the

Yearning For Eden/

process that forms the fabric which ties everything together in a meaningful relationship? And are we, intelligent life, not embedded in this fabric, a part of this choreographed dance of nature, an intentional unit within it, having a function that contributes to the meaning of it all?

Can it not be then, that life is bigger than we may have supposed? Can it be that life is designed as a part of a created system that is designed in eternity for eternity? And being a keystone part of that connected reality, would it not make sense that in preservation of that which has been brought into being, human life is designed to go on?

NATURE'S NECESSITY

What is the meaning of it all? Why does the cosmos exist? What is humanity's role in it? Is it all just happenstance, a fluke of mere chance? John Archibald Wheeler, former director of the Center for Theoretical Physics at the University of Texas at Austin, the man who proved that black holes exist, asks: How could the universe exist and make sense unless it were guaranteed to give rise at some point to life and mind and meaning? He raised the question, "Is man an unimportant bit of dust on an unimportant galaxy somewhere in the vastness of space?

Yearning For Eden/

He then answered his question, "No! The necessity to produce life lies at the center of the universe's whole machinery and design." Wheeler's belief is that the concept of a universe is meaningless unless there is a community of thinkers to observe it, and that community is impossible unless the universe is adapted from the start to give rise to life and mind.[5]

Having reviewed the knowledge discussed above, we can now address the questions: Why is it that we all have to feel that we are a part of something? What is the reason for this need for connection?

And we can formulate a reasonable answer: Is it not that we are designed for relationship? We are relational beings, part of a cosmic design that is a vast connectional system. This need to relate, to belong to, to function with, is built into our nature. It is not something that we can turn off and on. It is not a thing that is under our control, we did not design ourselves. It is integral to the definition of "human."

This need to be a part of is like hunger that is generated by the body's requirement for food. The very core of us hungers for this sense of completion by fitting into the "whole." Our human mechanism is not in its natural state when it is detached from the rest of its milieu. Lewis Thomas tells us, "The whole dear notion of oneself -- marvelous old free willed, free enterprising,

Yearning For Eden/

autonomous, independent, isolated island of a self -- is a myth."[6]

And we are not mere dust on an unimportant galaxy; we are not insignificant. We are intelligent life, a keystone, that brings meaning to the whole structure. The universe is the way it is because we are in it. The whole enterprise is adapted, from the beginning, to give rise to what we are. And without us that enterprise has no significance.

But, reciprocally, this system to which we add import also brings meaning to us. It is by functioning in it as we are designed to do that we find purpose for our own life. As we act in fulfillment of this purpose, in harmonic relationship with the whole fabric, we achieve a feeling of belonging that brings, in the very depth of our soul, a sense of peace and well-being. In that condition we are in a state of "loving relationship," in touch with self and others, not alienated from, and we are functioning so as to achieve the fullest potential of our humanity.

We can now turn to ancient tradition, passed down through thousands of years, to seek, in this regard, further enlightenment regarding this choreographed waltz of nature.

CHAPTER 4:
THE MEANING OF THE DANCE

Somewhere, back in the long eons of time, an ancient thinker contemplated the meaning of the presence of humankind in the vast expanse of an undefined universe. And as he sat, he penned on scroll the thoughts that played within his mind.

> O Lord, our Lord,
> How majestic is your name in all the earth!
> ...When I consider your heavens,
> the work of your fingers,
> the moon and the stars,
> which you have set in place,
> what is man that you are mindful of him,
> and the son of man that you care for him?
> You made him a little lower than the heavenly beings,
> and crowned him with glory and honor.
> You made him ruler over the works of your hands;
> you put everything under his feet...
> O Lord, our Lord,
> how majestic is your name in all the earth!
> (Psalm 8)

As a pastor and counselor, I cannot number the times I have heard the words, "Why am I here? I have nothing left to live for!" come to me through the lips of a depressed or grieving or otherwise distraught person. What are we that God is mindful of us? The question is ages old, women and men have been raising it and debating its answer throughout human history. How does humankind's experience with life, the wisdom that comes from "having done it" through the course of history, answer the question?

ANCIENT WISDOM

How do we confirm the view that was presented in the last chapter of this vast cosmos of which we are this important part? How do we corroborate this understanding of our position in it and our relationship with it?

We cannot stand outside it, off from it, looking into it, because we are embedded in it. Yet even before we acquired the scientific knowledge that we have today an ancient people had gained this perception of a unified creation and an understanding of their place in it. Where did their conception of life and what it is a part of come from?

The Hebrew people's concepts came from a Source revealed to them as "I AM WHO I AM." This Being was also known as Yahweh (Lord), an infinitely perfect Deity, the creative cause of the universe, the intelligent author of what is observed as "nature," the power they knew as God. This Creator God was not a Being discovered, or known through intellectual reasoning, but rather a self-revealing Deity who came to them as "the God of your father, the God of Abraham, the God of Isaac, the God of Jacob" (Ex. 3:6).

And this Source opened to them a wisdom that could not come from their eyes alone, could not be conceived solely through their finite reason. There was a phenomenon we call "revelation" involved. Revelation, while it goes beyond empirically provable reasoning, is not necessarily opposed to reason. These ancients recorded that wisdom, which unfolds in the pages of Scripture, opening with the pronouncement, "In the beginning God created the heavens and the earth." A single Author of a single system.

We find in Scripture no questions about where God came from or explanation of His existence. He is simply accepted by these ancient people as the "one who is." Paul Huber in his book *Creation for What?* points out what is logically true: "We created beings could not hope to be able to explain our Creator, His origin, or His reason for being, any more than the electronic computer can explain its creator, or the vase its potter."[1]

Huber goes on to discuss why it is not valid to ask such questions as "Where did God come from? and "What was there before God?" These queries make no sense, Huber indicates, "because concepts of time, space, and so forth are only applicable during the period of physical existence, but not before or after."[2] In other words, time and space and such concepts exist only after the creation, with the beginning of history. They are not applicable to the spiritual realm that is outside of this history.

In the Christian church, St. Augustine and St. Ansi do not approach such questions either, but simply state that "in order to understand one must believe." However both these early saints of the church insist that by reason the existence of God can be demonstrated.

Yearning For Eden/

St. Anselm formulated the argument which starts neither from things that we can make sense of, nor from the possession of any truth. His reasoning begins with the concept of who God is and states: "God is that than which nothing greater can be conceived; and, therefore, God must exist, since if He did not exist, He would not be that than which nothing greater can be conceived. If, then, God is that than which nothing greater can be conceived, existence cannot be taken away from Him, He must exist."[3]

SCIENCE AND FAITH

Is this ancient wisdom concerning the existence of God who designed and brought into being this cosmic system incompatible with the science of our day? Stephen W. Hawking, the brilliant theoretical physicist, states in his book *A Brief History of Time*, "The whole history of science has been the gradual realization that events do not happen in an arbitrary manner, but that they reflect a certain underlying order, which may or may not be divinely inspired"[4]

Paul Huber, a research scientist mentioned above, writes,

> Science has accepted on the basis of historic constancy and repeatability all physical laws and natural properties of the universe as being absolute and complete - yet cannot explain why these laws and properties came to be constituted as they are... It has been quite possible for the scientific disciplines to readily accept all this type of evidence on the "faith" that it somehow came to be, and yet it has been impossible to also accept on faith the overwhelming circumstantial evidence that there must be a "consciousness" present in

Yearning For Eden/

> the universe responsible for such a fantastically remarkable creation.[5]

The most prominent theory concerning the beginning of the universe held among scientists today is termed the "Big Bang" theory. Lately there have been momentous findings to support this view which holds that there was a creative moment at which time the universe began. This theory has provided a common ground for religion and science. Speaking from its prospective Rev. Frederick B. Burnett, a science historian and director of the Trinity Institute in New York City, says, "There was a beginning and there will be an end."

Stephen Hawking, a foremost physicist, says that if this theory is correct, "It would be very difficult to explain why the universe should have begun in this way, except as an act of a God who intended to create beings like us"[6]

Genesis is the Hebraic book of beginnings and in this Scripture these ancient people have preserved their inspired view of God's creative act. In its first pages they have described the ordering of chaos and the origin of light, sky, land mass and seas, vegetation, heavenly bodies, living creatures of sea and land, and finally, made in the Creator's own image, man and woman. Humanity was the keystone of this creation, imbued with a spirit -- in His image -- granted powers of reason and free-will beyond any other creatures.

Into humanity's hands was given dominion to subdue and rule over what had been made on earth.

Hundreds of years later, coming through these same Hebrew people was a further revelation reinforcing and elaborating the original wisdom. Jesus of Nazareth, who by his crucifixion and resurrection was authenticated in the eyes of many as the Messiah of God, referred to God's creative act as fact.[7] For believers this is like getting truth "from the horse's mouth." The basis for this acceptance is a faith that knows that random chance cannot be the origin of such magnificent structure and accepts the reality of a Creator who reveals Himself to mortals for His own purposes.

Paul, a chosen disciple and evangelist of Jesus Christ, indicates, "For since the creation of the world God's invisible qualities -- his eternal power and divine nature -- have been clearly seen, being understood from what has been made..." (Ro. 1:20). Thus Paul is able to state, "By faith we understand that the universe was formed at God's command, so that what is seen was not made out of what was visible" (Heb. 11:3).

If we give, heed to this ancient wisdom that comes from a Source whose sight is beyond the purview of our own humanity, we gain a perspective of things that lay outside our finite ken. From the wisdom revealed by that Creating Power, we gain corroboration for what the insights of science point us toward:

That there was a creative moment.

That it would be very difficult to explain such a beginning, except as an act of God who intended to create beings like us.

That there is a harmony to the entire network, a functional unity conducted in the context of observable natural law.

Yearning For Eden/

That we are not an insignificant part of that system, but a part from which it derives a reason for being and from which, reciprocally, our existence takes meaning.

And that we are relational beings, created to function as a harmonious element within that network of which we are this keystone piece.

YOU, ME, AND THE WHOLE UNIVERSE

If then, we see this case for a unitary cosmos, a single life enterprise existing as an articulated "whole," brought into being by a Creator who designed it with purpose, what does that tell us about our functioning within it? Although we are the keystone piece, intelligent life made in the image of the Creator, we are only "a" piece of that "whole." Our purpose is embedded in the purpose of that totality, not the other way around.

We, although a key element of this reason for its being, are not "the reason." If we look again to that wisdom revealed to those ancient peoples and recorded in Scripture, the central purpose of the creation is unveiled: God acted that it might work to the Creator's glory and honor.

Speaking of Jesus Christ as the visible image of God, scripture says,

> For by him all things were created: things in heaven and on earth, visible and invisible, whether thrones or powers or rulers or authorities; all things were created by him *and for him*" (Col. 1:16, Italics mine).

Yearning For Eden/

The ultimate reason for the universe is to serve the purpose of the Creator, it is "for Him." Humanity has a central role in that purpose. "I will be their God and they will be my people" (Jer. 31:33). So we then are made for relationship with the Creator. The universe is the system in which we are placed to carry on that relationship with God.

Women and men are the intelligent life who can observe and appreciate that system, which benefits their existence, and be the vessels through which that glory is given. "They will be my people." In reciprocity, that Creator who has given life will support and sustain life. "I will be their God."

A GOOD THING TURNED BAD

But something is wrong. Things are not as they should be if the concepts presented above are operating. The earth on which we live is not a harmonic place; the world is full of strife and contention. People are not at peace with each other. Shalom is a hope for which most of us long but few seem to have found. Our daily news reports tell us that humanity is estranged from each other and in violation of the environment which supports our life. If the Creator's plan for what has been brought into being is to unfold in the context of relationship, loving (agape) relationship, then something is not functioning as it was designed.

Could the problem be that we are the problem? Are we living in a state of alienation from that system? Are we separated from and not in tune with the purpose for which we were given life? Listen to the observation of Albert Einstein whose theory of relativity has been the basis for our understanding of the universe since he formulated it.

> A human being is part of the whole called by us the universe, a part limited in time and space. He experiences himself, his thoughts and feelings as something separated from the rest, a kind of optical delusion of his consciousness. This delusion is a kind of prison for us, restricting us to our personal desires and to affection for a few persons nearest to us. Our task must be to free ourselves from this prison by widening our circle of compassion to embrace all living creatures and the whole of nature in its beauty.[8]

Have we attempted to force things to conform to our own individual wills in a misconceived idea that we are the masters? Have we thought that we are in control, that we can stand off from the designed fabric of creation and set our own purposes for life, implement those purposes with our own pattern for living, instead of conforming to the Originator's plan? And is this misconception not a very old idea with deep roots in humanity's history? Listen to Isaiah, a prophet of Israel, as he speaks to those ancient people,

> You turn things upside down, as if the potter were thought to be like the clay!
> Shall what is formed say to him who formed it,
> "He didn't make me?"
> Can the pot say to the potter,
> "He knows nothing?" (Isaiah 29:16).

Humanity's arrogance is addressed by those ancients in what they record as the Creator's somewhat sarcastic response to those who would make themselves His equal.

Yearning For Eden/

> Where were you when I laid the earth's foundations? Tell me, if you understand, who marked off its dimensions? Surely you know! Who stretched its measuring line? On what were its footings set, who laid its cornerstone...? (Job 38:4-6).

From a more modern stance Lewis Thomas in his award winning book *The Lives of a Cell* observes,

> The oldest, easiest to swallow idea was that the earth was man's personal property, a combination of garden, zoo, bank vault, and energy source, placed at our disposal to be consumed, ornamented, or pulled apart as we wished... In the last few years we were wrenched away from this way of looking at it, and arrived at something like general agreement that we had it wrong. We still argue the details, but it is conceded almost everywhere that we are not the masters of nature that we thought ourselves; we are as dependent on the rest of life as are the leaves or midges or fish. We are part of the system. One way to put it is that the earth is a loosely formed, spherical organism, with all its parts in symbiosis.[9]

In our arrogance, over eons of time, we may have forgotten who we are, where our life came from, why we exist, what the meaning and purpose of life is, and where we are headed.

FREE WILL AND LOVE

If in fact there is such a Creative Power who choreographed this dance of nature to function in rhythmic harmony, why would that Being allow humanity to turn from the orchestrated score and detach itself from it, as we seem to have done? Why were we not programmed in such a way that we would have no choice but to play our role, as that was designed to be, in this great extravaganza? The answer is, "We are not ants!"

If relationship with us, loving relationship, is the desire of the Creator and the goal of His work, then His centerpieces in the creation must have the capacity to love. So women and men were made in the image of God, who by his act of creating and sustaining life is the very definition of agape. We were created to have the capacity to give and receive love.

This capacity to live in loving relationship is the hallmark of our humanity. But, by definition, love must be freely given. To love it is necessary to have the power to choose to love. And if this power to choose is granted, then attendant with that power is the ability to choose not to love. It cannot be otherwise!

So perhaps we are the problem! If we have used our freedom to chose to detach ourselves from the fabric of which we are part and parcel, then our detachment is of our own doing. If we have desired to be the gods of our own life, then we have, by our own volition, moved against the grain of the creation's design. Instead of loving relationship, we have chosen a self-centered, individual course and in so doing have become alienated from the Creator and His eternal purpose, from each other, and from the entire system that has been put into place.

A "CATCH 22"

When we are out of synchrony with the design mode of the creation, we are then in denial of our nature. We were created in the image of the Creator with the capacity to give and receive love. Our human machinery is built to function in connection with a symbiotic system whose components are a Designer, other beings like ourselves, and an environment conducive to life. When we act in a manner that violates the design and purpose of this system, we become disconnected from it.

This means we become dysfunctional, we malfunction, because we are not operating in accordance with the blueprint. We can deny the manner in which we were created to function, because we have a free will, the power to choose to do that. But we cannot turn off our nature, we did not create what we are.

When we choose to put ourselves outside of the harmonic design of this eternal system, we deny ourselves the sense of connection and fulfillment for which, in our unhappiness, we long. And we burden ourselves with worry about death, which we can see only as an ending. We are unable to view it confidently as a transition, because we have disconnected ourselves from the place where life is designed to continue.

Then we live in a kind of "catch 22," desperately searching for a solace we cannot find. We cannot find it because we have lost touch with that part of our humanity that can lead us to it. It is the part of us that can admit its own finiteness and vulnerability, a part that can experience dependency, a part that can open us to connection and agape, a part that can admit that we cannot be the god of our life.

So deep within our humanity there is an unrest, a longing for the peace and contentment that comes from knowing "God

Yearning For Eden/

is in His heaven and all is right with the world." It is a memory of an archaic state of shalom that lives in the fiber of what we are, lost but not forgotten, somehow retained in the substance of what we were created to be.

But we know that all is not right with the world and it is not right because women and men are not in harness with the eternal plan. We may concede that "God is in His heaven," but we have challenged the Creator's authority. We want to be the gods of our own life, create our own design, fashion our own goals, and pursue them in our own individualistic way. This brings conflict and discord as we bump against each other, pushing and shoving to satisfy our own needs and appetites. It spawns an anxiety concerning our mortality, because our finite vision cannot see beyond our own death. Disconnected from the system and on our own, we are unable to generate any certainty about the dimensions of life and where its path is taking us.

We long for personal fulfillment. Yet we fight against the surrender of self that will make us part of a creation which is designed to function in peace through loving relationship. We stumble about chasing power, wealth, and possessions that fail, again and again, to assuage that deep inner need for connection and shalom. In our desire to change the plan, to make ourselves the masters that we are not, we fail to accede to what Carlo Corretto points out in his book *Why O Lord*?

> There is only God! This is the cornerstone of the kingdom. Nothing can disturb the design, the perfection of the kingdom, nothing can change the will of God. At the very most you can remain on the

> outside. But everything is so arranged that to stay on the outside is a continuous hell... [10]

Again the ancients beat us to this truth, for when Moses brought the Law to those Hebrew people he told them that God commanded, "I am the Lord your God... You shall have no other gods before me" (Ex. 20:2-3).

But if this is an acceptable understanding of the human situation, we have only just scratched the surface. How can we be a part of something as remote as a distant star, as huge as eternity, and as near as our neighbor? How can we be here on earth, physically embedded in this universe, and yet be outside of the system? What are the mechanics of connection; by what chords are we to be tied together in loving relationship?

What does all this have to do with how we feel when we get up in the morning, how we function through the day, the sense of loneliness that can overtake us even in a crowd, the inner feeling of contentment that we cannot sustain, the monotony of daily routine that becomes a bore, the failure of "getting" and "having" to bring a lasting satisfaction to life, and our anxiety about death?

PART III:
AND WE'RE CONNECTED TO THE DIVINE

Love is the doorway through which the human soul passes from selfishness to service and from solitude to kinship with all mankind.

Anonymous

CHAPTER 5: UNDERSTANDING IT

But how can God be in us? In me? A part of my humanity? Is it possible for another being to be a part of what we are, a part of our selfhood? And when we say to a loved one who is going off to some taxing experience on which we cannot accompany him/her, "I'll be with you in spirit," is there any reality to that? Are these some sentimental notions, figures of speech that have no basis in the mechanics of our humanity?

Or is there a "spiritual connection" that can be made? Is there a mechanism which functions within our human instrumentality that does not depend upon physical presence? Can there be a process which makes such mystical phenomena a possibility? Can we harbor within us a sprig of the spirit of an intimate friend or other loved one? Can we carry with us as a part of our being the Being of God? Can these objects be a real and functioning part of who we are? Some answers to these questions would be helpful in accepting the reality of a Divine connection.

Actually there is a model through which we may understand that these questions can all have a positive answer. It may challenge our sensibilities, because most of us are grounded in the world of the physical. But this model plots a psychological reality that while not physical, you cannot put it under a microscope to examine it, is as real as the tissues of the body that can be examined in that way.

To understand that model will require that we venture into some psychological theory. It will be a superficial journey, for our need here is not the detail of a textbook. But the excursion will contain the main way stations, so that we can lay out the path to our destination. Through an overview of object relations theory, it will be possible to construct an understanding of how some mystical phenomena of the spiritual can be a reality for us.

If you will bear with me through this small bit of detail, we will emerge with some insights as to how the "self" develops within the psyche, how we construct and carry with us images of significant people in our lives, how these become a real part of that "self" who we are, and something of the content and functioning of our unconscious. Our reward for journeying through this technical detail, which I promise to keep as simple and brief as possible, will be the development of a concept of how God can realistically be an integral part of who we are. How God can be "in us."

We will also see how it might be literally possible to be with someone "in spirit" when you are not physically together. In doing this, we will draw upon sound psychological theory whose development comes through the contributions of Frued, Jung, Abraham, Klein, Fairbain, Winnicott and Bion.

IMAGES THAT PLAY IN THE MIND

As we are well aware, the mind has the capacity to deal with things that are not physical entities -- thoughts, ideas, emotions, dreams, representations of things not present, and so forth. The artist can put on canvas a picture that he envisions in his head. The composer can write down a melody that he hears in his mind. The engineer can draw plans for a structure he conceives through mentally processing a vast array of data.

This ability is not present in the infant. That is why, for babies, things out of sight do not exist. So when mother leaves the room it is tantamount to abandonment for the very young child. The infant does not yet have the capacity to carry a mental image of mother which assures the child of mother's continued existence. As we grow we develop the capacity to deal with our world mentally rather than simply through direct concrete experience. Things do not have to be physically present for us to deal with them.

Our capacity for language is utilized to enable us to handle reality through a system of symbols. Each word has a corresponding "object" stored in our brain, so that when it is used we can picture that which is being referenced. Thus when someone speaks to us of "chair," we have stored in our memory a whole inventory of different kinds of chairs that we have experienced.

When that word is used we can search our inventory for a particular kind of chair. We can mentally manipulate the object to fully examine its characteristics. We can do all sorts of creative thinking about decorating it, redesigning it, or picturing it in various locations in a room. Stored in our memory is a whole world of objects and experiences to which we can relate through mental imaging and language.

Now I review this information with which we are all acquainted, because it is similar to the psychological process which we are about to discuss. As we grow, the person who we are, and are becoming, develops through a process that involves the incorporation of "representations" of other people. These images, which psychologists call "objects," are representations of the perceived characteristics of significant people who have been in a position to have a dramatic impact on our life.

Parents, or those who have raised us, are the most important significant others in our lives. Their personalities, as we see them, and the kind of experiences we have in our relationships with them have the greatest impact on the person we become. And of the two parents, "mother" takes the primary position of significance. But other people like relatives with whom we may have a special relationship, teachers, friends, heroes, and so forth can also be significant in the development of our own personhood. We cannot physically carry these people around with us, so we form images of them which we internalize as "objects."

But these images are different than the chair whose "picture" we incorporated in our memory. With these significant others the representation is not just a picture of their physical appearance. Because of their special impact on our life, we incorporate elements of their personality construct, as we perceive that personality, into our developing "self." These "objects" are not simply recorded in memory, but become a functioning part of who we are. Our ego, that entity who we identify as "me," is composed in part of these incorporated "objects."

PICTURING THE SELF

So we can envision that "me" as being composed of a central core with these assimilated aspects of "significant others" clustered within that self. When we exhibit certain traits that are "just like her mother," or "so like his father," they come not from the genes, but from these internalized elements of mother's and father's personhood. We do all of this not by conscious thought. The process is carried out and the "objects" are internalized by the unconscious part of our mind.

The first person we get to know is mother and she is a key individual in determining who we become. Therefore, it is elements of mother's person that are first incorporated as part of our developing self. Our unconscious internalizes this "object" so as not to lose mother. In that way she becomes a part of us.

Our developing perceptions, attitudes, values, and behaviors are influenced by this representation of "mom" that has been taken into our unconsciousness and has become part of our personhood.

This internalization takes place around our perceptions of mother's loving response to us. Love is formative for human beings. We crave it and need it, as we do food and water when we are hungry and thirsty. If our need is satisfied we are soothed, contented, and satisfied. When mother acts to sooth us, the infant views this behavior as "good." When mother's behavior does not satisfy this craving for love, it disturbs the infant and the behavior is viewed as "bad."

So the infant experiences mother as both satisfying, "good," and unsatisfying, "bad." Eventually we build up a characterization of mother based on our experiences with her. And this is the substance of what we preserve in the "object" of her that we internalize. The "object" is the unconscious perceptions we have of mother. That image is built up over the years, layer by layer, on top of the initial representation we incorporated.

In similar fashion images of father and other individuals who come to be significant influences in our lives form. These are internalized as aspects of our ego. In this way some of their characteristics come to be reflected in our own personality. Who we become is literally an amalgam of who we see our self as, our core "self," and those by whom we have been significantly influenced. The "self" is our image of who we are, and includes the "objects" we have internalized and their related affects upon us.

PICTURING THE MIND

Now as we have said, all of this does not happen by conscious calculation. We do not intentionally think to do these things. It is the unconscious part of our mind that operates to bring about these internalizations. That unconsciousness, Carl Jung discovered, has two aspects. There is a part that contains material that is closely associated with our personal life. This part he labeled the personal unconscious. It is the part of the mind that deals with the internalization of the "objects" which we just discussed. It also harbors such things as ideas and impressions temporarily lost to memory, as well as thoughts too objectionable to the conscious mind to be acknowledged.

But through his study of the content and meaning of dreams, Jung became aware that there was a second, deeper layer of the unconscious mind. This part he called the collective unconscious. He found that it contained material associated with universal human experience that goes beyond anything that we might have been directly associated with in our own time or culture. In presenting what follows, I am discussing what I have previously written about in Living With God in Loss.[1]

Jung found that there was a communication that took place between the conscious part of our mind and these aspects of the unconscious. The mechanisms for this exchange when asleep are our dreams. But also, when awake, the communication goes on through such phenomena as the "Freudian slip" of tongue or behavior, whims, the prodding of our conscience, premonitions, intuition, and serendipity which opens new potentials for us. Even the development of a neurotic condition or experiencing deep-seated fears, anxieties, and depression -- which are signals of a malfunction of our mental health -- are examples of the influence of the unconscious on our conscious functioning.

This layer of our mind that operates outside of our consciousness, Jung discovered, always works to maintain health and growth. He found that if we consciously discard or ignore things that are vital to our life and growth, such that they completely disappear from awareness, the unconscious will develop compensating counteraction to the jeopardizing behavior. Thus the impulse of the unconscious is always to guide and empower the positive development of the self which resides in the conscious. The communications that we receive from the unconscious, then, always have the intent of propelling us toward honesty, truthfulness, and reality.

The obvious questions that arise now are: Where does this content and impulse of the unconscious come from -- the heritage; wisdom; orientation toward health and growth; espousal of honesty, truth, and reality as the only perspectives from which to operate; the warning of uncomfortableness; the balancing and compensating for our own unhealthy tendencies; the urge to become more than we are? If it does not emanate from our own conscious thought, what "mind" generates such things from within our own being? Through what agency is our personhood connected with all humanity over time and across space: with cultures which are personally unknown to us, with intelligence that cannot be accounted for by our own learning or experience?

How can we account for such a phenomenon? It has to come from a realm which overarches the place and time of the physical sphere in which we live. It must have an omnipresence that resides within each of us at the same time. It must generate a communication link that we cannot explain with our physics. It must be the ultimate proponent of life, its author and sustainer.

What mind can that be but that of the Being who is Creator of life and universe? Who can that be but the Power we apprehend as Almighty God? Only that which we name God is transcendent Spirit, existing beyond time and the cosmos, yet being a condescending Presence that is with us and in us. Only such a Universal Consciousness can be cognizant of all human history; but exceed that history, be outside of it. Only that which is the very definition of love can exhibit the unswerving, self-giving bent to protect and promote life. Such a Source must have the character of love; its operational mode must be grace.

MADE IN THE IMAGE OF LOVE

Now to understand how this omnipresent, omniscient Power can be with us and in each of us, all at the same time, we can recall our discussion of internal objects. In that material we saw how our mind operates to incorporate into our developing "self" our perceived representations of mother, father, and other significant people who have a pronounced influence upon us. And we understand that those internalized "objects" become a functional part of us. They are influential in molding who we are -- the way we perceive our world, how we think, what we value, the attitudes we hold, the behaviors we exhibit, the traits, mannerisms and emotions which we reflect.

These representations exist in a very real way as part of who we are, even though they are not physical substances. Those "others" are incorporated into our ego as "objects." And all of this occurs in a process of which we are not consciously aware. It is a part of that aspect of our mind which Jung labeled the personal unconscious.

Now we can relate this information to what Scripture is telling us when it says, "Let us make man in our image, in our likeness... (Gen. 1:26). Does this teaching mean we have the physical attributes of our Creator? Does it imply that when we look into a mirror the reflection we see is that of God? No one really believes that. Then does it mean that we have all the capabilities of our Creator -- that we are omnipotent, omniscient, omnipresent? We know for a fact that we are not all powerful, all knowing, and able to be present everywhere at the same time. So what does being made in the image of God really mean?

Well what does Scripture tell us that God is? What is the essence of this Being who revelation reveals as the Parent of life and the Creator of all that we apprehend? Scripture says that "...God is love" (1 John 4:8). Put in another way, it is telling us that God's essence is love. So if we are made in this

Creator's likeness, we are made in the image of a Being whose quintessence is love!

But love is not a physical thing that we can be molded to look like. Love is a condition of relationship, a disposition toward others. If we are made in Love's image, then there must be something designed into our human substance that has given us the disposition to give and receive love. Somewhere in the essence of what we are there is an image of a Being that inclines us to engage in relationship in the way God relates, to be loving. If the capacity to love is designed into our humanity, then there is some tangible element in our constitution that disposes us to be like God in our relationships -- to "feel" like God feels toward us. Being made in the image of God has to mean that the loving character of God is planted within us, somewhere in the very substance of what we are. But where is it? And what is it? What kind of reality are we dealing with here that is not physical and yet is a part of our essence? Here we must retrace our steps to the discussion we had of the mind.

The mind is not a physical substance, yet it is very real. The mind utilizes the brain and all other parts of our physique, but it is more than the physical parts in which it has its life. We cannot put our finger on our consciousness, nor on the unconscious. We cannot look at them with our eyes or see them on an X-ray film. Yet they are a part of us.

We have seen how our developing "ego" incorporates images of our parents and significant others into itself. But these "objects" which we internalize are not physical commodities.

They are ethereal characterizations of our mind, which itself is ethereal. Yet all these things are real. They function and their operation is observable in the affects that they produce. That reality affects who we are, how we perceive our world, what we believe, what we value, and how we act and react in our living.

Within that deeper part of our unconscious mind -- which is known to contain material that goes beyond our own time and our own personal experience -- can there be implanted an ethereal "object" which is the image of God? Can there be a "representation" within this collective unconscious, not that we have internalized in the way we do those of our parents, but an "object" which resides in our mind as do the images of those significant others that form a part of who we are?

If this were inlaid as an act of creation, would it not give meaning to Scripture's teaching that we are made in the "image of God?" Could it be a likeness of our Creator, not a physical resemblance, but an ethereal aspect of the Divine essence which embodies the character of love? Can such an image, although not a physical entity, be as real as the psychic representations of the "others" which we have unconsciously internalized as segments of our own ego? Would not this construct, housed within our mind, be there as a built-in aspect of our humanity, of who we are? Does this not explain how God can be in each of us at the same time, just as a parent is an incorporated "object" existing simultaneously as part of the ego of each sibling in a family?

DISCOVERING AN OBJECT LOST

But if this is the case, why are people not the loving creatures that this construct would imply we would be? If this is an accurate hypothesis, why is it universally true that human beings have great difficulty living together in peaceful coexistence.

Could not this implanted image be part of ourselves with which we have lost touch? Could it be a part that we have denied exists, because we can no longer recognize the spiritual element of our humanity? Can it be a part from which we have turned away from, even though investigators have seen the evidence of its presence reflecting material which goes beyond our own time and personal experience; working always in the direction of preserving life and promoting growth? Can this not be the disposition to loving relationship that we have lost, the feeling toward others that God has toward us? Could it be a memory trace with which we have difficulty reconnecting, a recollection that brings into focus an honest perspective of who we are and where we have come from?

Is it this for which our inner heart craves as an ancient remembrance of a relationship human beings had in a far-distant past? Having lost this connection, do we feel so exposed and alone that we cower in fear, using denial as a blanket to cover the finitude and vulnerability we do not want to face?

What has been presented is a construct which could exist in a part of our humanity that is as real as our own mind. It explains how God can be with us and in us, there to affect who we are and what we become. It describes an operation much like that in which the elements of our parent's personality, through the "objects" of them which we have internalized, affect the person we are.

WHERE'S THE PROOF?

What I have "supposed" above is not provable by the scientific method. There is no irrefutable data to advance that can document it with airtight certainty. An X-ray of the brain cannot disclose the anatomy and content of the mind. If God, during that creative moment which gave birth to life, incorporated an image of the Divine Self within us, there is no way to substantiate that fact beyond all doubt. If that implant can function from within the collective unconscious, in similar fashion to the "objects" of our parents and significant others that get incorporated into our personal unconscious, it is beyond scientific verification.

But all the anecdotal evidence from human history points to something that does operate in a fashion which has been described above. There is the testimony of scripture that declares that we are made in the likeness of our Creator. There are the accounts of this Presence in scripture which report what women and men through centuries of time have experienced: the inner voice that has spoken, the dreams and visions that have conveyed messages, the irresistible impulses that have guided people in one direction or another, the thoughts which give rise to great acts.

There is the personal witness of those who live in our own time which attests to the same kind of encounters. Some of these dramatic stories will be presented in Chapter Seven. There are those individuals in whose lives we see reflected a love that is an emulation of the Divine. These are not always prominent figures like a Mother Teresa or an Albert Schweitzer. That love is modeled by some who come from our own neighborhoods. These are everyday people like Susan, who we will meet in Chapter Ten. Their constant closeness to God is evident in the peace and serenity they exude, even through the many stresses that come with life. They live in that state of shalom which is so notable that we comment about it.

Psychologists, psychiatrists, and counselors have noted an aspect of our mind that they cannot explain, but whose presence they see. Carl Jung observed and wrote: "everything living strives for wholeness." There is an innervating energy, a healthy ingredient which functions within the human psyche on behalf of our survival and growth. Eric Berne, a psychiatrist known as the father of transactional analysis, wrote of it. "But there is something beyond all this -- some force which drives people to grow, progress, and do better..."[2]

And this positive influence affects not only our psychological functioning but empowers us physically. Scott Peck, who is also a psychiatrist and writer, comments about it. "We can therefore say the same thing about physical disorders that we said about mental disorders: There is a force, the mechanisms of which we do not fully understand, that seems to operate routinely in most people to protect and encourage their physical health even under the most adverse conditions."[3]

There is no concrete proof of what I have hypothesized above. But the testimony of scripture, and the experience of ordinary people and trained professionals over the course of human history attest to the fact that some Force, of which we have little or no knowledge, functions as a composite element of our human nature. What other reality is there that could display such power and love for us, except that of the Being we call God?

And is it not reasonable that such a Presence should operate within us in similar fashion to other "objects" that get incorporated into our self-system? It provides a reality to Scripture's teaching: "Then God said, 'Let us make man in our image, in our likeness...'" (Gen. 1:26). It provides a model for understanding how God can be in us, a functional part of our humanity, that enables us to be in touch with the eternal precincts now.

But that Divine Essence within can have no benefit if we are not open to its being there. If we deny its presence, if we ignore its reality, then we will not accredit its communications. We will discount the credence of those signals and ignore their message. For another aspect of our humanity is the free-will with which we are endowed. This power to choose enables us to act in love. Love, by definition, must be freely given. So if we are designed to be loving creatures, we must have the ability to choose to love. But at the same time, that freedom of choice provides the opportunity for us to turn away from loving relationship.

DENYING THE CONNECTION

Denial is a psychological function that is a part of our human repertory. We use it to avoid accepting traumatic or distasteful reality which we do not want to acknowledge: "I don't believe it!" "She would not do that." "That never happened." If the Presence of God within us is a threat to the Great Lie, that we can be the gods of our own life, which the human race is attempting to perpetuate, then we have both reason and mechanism for discounting and ignoring that Presence. We can deny the image of Love that resides within us.

And the evidence that we have leads us to conclude that most of the human race, through its history, has denied the spiritual realities of its nature. We've done that so as to hang on to that fabricated illusion that we are the gods of our own life. As a result, we have lost touch with the Spirit that lives within us as the Image in which we were created. We have done that for so long that the God-part in us appears to us not to be there at all. Thus we have lost the sense of who we are and the memory of from whence we came. We are out of touch with that which is our empowerment for loving relationship. So we have become alienated from the Creative Force that parented life, from those with whom we share life, and from the universe which supports our life.

Lacking the connection with Love, we have evolved into creatures that no longer understand what love is. We are left with only the ability to look inward to self, becoming selfish in nature. With that focus, we are no longer able to see that our neighbor is "me" -- of the same substance, hoping for the same dreams, having the same aspirations, exhibiting the same needs, a part of the same team. We do not see our "sameness." We see only "difference." We have lost our sense of family.

And seeing "difference" we envy, we are jealous, we ostracize, we live for the day to satisfy our own appetites, and we kill each other in war. We do not know peace, because we have lost touch with that which is the basis for all serenity, loving relationship. Instead of living as family, we live as individuals. By our denial, we have cut ourselves off from that which is the essence of our humanity and have lost the image of the persons we were created to be.

If God then is a reality that exists within our humanity that can affiliate with us then how can this play out in people's lives? Some examples follow in the next chapter.

CHAPTER 6: BELIEVING IT

Dan was a church friend of mine who was looking for the truths about eternal life. That is not the way that he would have phrased it, but I believe that was the basic reality of his search.

Dan attended a Christian church, even though he confessed that he was not sure that he was really a Christian. He explained to me, one evening as we sat in his home, that he was not convinced that there really was a God. There were so many bad things that happened in the world, Dan said, that he could not conceive of a loving Creator making such a world and allowing it to continue to exist as it is.

But despite his reservation, he wasn't really sure about his position. There was unrest within him, a discontent with the idea that life had no meaning other than what we decide to do with it between birth and death. There was an emptiness inside him that needed to be filled; it blocked the way to the assurance that is mother to the contentment that he sought. So he searched for God in a church where he wasn't sure that he belonged, looking for a Being he really did not believe existed, in the ultimate hope that he would achieve the peace he had not yet found.

THE NECESSITY OF CONVICTION

As we talked that evening Dan, who was a very intelligent man, told me he needed proof before he could fully give himself to faith. Dan was a man of facts and logical reason. He did not, at some point, want to find that he had been made the fool. "Suppose," he said, "that you get to the end and find you've been snookered."

Dan had things reversed, "the cart before the horse," but didn't realize it. He was looking for a belief that was already proven factually, laid out in irrefutable detail. But faith is irrelevant in the presence of such a condition. There is no need for faith when incontrovertible fact has already substantiated belief. Faith is conviction that does not rest on logical proof. Scripture says: "Now faith is being sure of what we hope for and certain of what we do not see" (Heb. 11:1).

So Dan's tactic is flawed. With his approach to the matter he can never achieve that condition of trust which will produce the contentment and assurance of eternity he seeks. Dan's dilemma is the predicament of a vast number of people in the world.

To find Eden, we must start with some conviction that heaven exists. The journey to the garden starts with a faith that the place is real. Those who search for lost treasure start with some belief that there is something to find. There may be an old tale that carries some sense of authenticity, a resurrected news account, or some other indication that there is something to be found.

Scripture's way of telling us this is in the teaching, "No one comes to the Father except through me. If you really knew me, you would know my Father as well" (John 14:6-7). These words of Jesus become clear when we put them in the context of the broader message he was bringing: What I am teaching you comes from the Creator whose child you are; a relationship with this heavenly Father happens only when you believe the message of which I am the courier.

In other words the lesson is: the search for the Divine connection must start with the faith that God exists and is sending this word about relationship with Him through this ministry. The Sender, the message, and the Bearer are all bound together.

THE FOUNDATION OF CONVICTION

The basis for faith is simply our experience with life. It begins with a growing awareness of our own inability to create what we are and what we are a part of. It matures as we recognize that such coordinated grandeur cannot be happenstance, some loving Universal Intelligence brought forth the life we have. Then the desire to connect with that Love and relate with it can develop.

Achieving a faith is a mystical process, beyond description that comes through personal experience. Recognizing our limitedness, we perceive a Power who has brought all life into being and the cosmos in which life exists. We have named that Power God.

Faith is not a rare phenomenon, but neither is it a universal trait. In 1990 the Gallup Organization published the People's Religion: American Faith in the 90's. In it they reported that 94 percent of the public believe in God. Ninety percent pray and 88 percent believe God loves them. In 1991 George Gallup, Jr. reported that a surprising forty-one percent of the nation's teenagers go to organized Bible studies. Sixty-four percent of Americans believe Jesus Christ rose from the dead and is a living presence. One and a half billion of the Earth's population claim to be Christians. Faith is also evident through the lives of all those people who follow the many other religions of the world. In fact, anthropology tells us that there is no known society through history that has not had a belief in some spirit world.

BELIEF MAKES A DIFFERENCE

Faith, though not based on proof, does have a tangible reality about it. That pragmatic aspect is revealed by experiences such as reported by Captain John L. Trestrake. He was the pilot of TWA Flight 847 that was hijacked and held hostage with its crew and passengers in Beirut, Lebanon. For days upon end they were detained at gunpoint, enduring incredible living conditions, suffering both physical and psychological abuse. Captain Trestrake testified that it was his faith that got him through that terrible ordeal.

His witness is like that of many who were held in Iran for almost a year when the American Embassy in Teheran was besieged. One of those was Colonel David Roeder who was held in solitary confinement for much of that time. After the event, he told Norman Vincent Peale to tell people: "The idea of God being real, of God being close to you when you need him is an absolute fact. Not fantasy. Not poetry. Fact. He was with me. He was there. Without Him I couldn't have made it." Later, Terry Anderson and others who were held through the 1980's by Middle East terrorists would make similar statements after their release.

This mystic power that belief displays is also witnessed to by people dealing with the ordinary traumas of life. Representative is a woman whose letter was published in the Ann Landers newspaper column. The woman had had two mastectomies because of breast cancer, her teenaged son had committed suicide, and her husband left her for another woman. After detailing these losses she wrote: "Above all it was believing in God and having faith in myself (that got me through). If I could go from a living hell to peace and serenity, anyone can." Human history is replete with such testimony.

LESSONS FROM ANOTHER REALM

When the search for God and the Divine connection begins from the platform of faith, a conviction that there is something to be found, new possibilities for exploration and understanding are opened. Revelation becomes a rich source of guidance that is not there if we are closed to the reality of the spiritual aspects of life.

For example, the revelation of Scripture is analogous to finding an old treasure map with a set of directions from some old prospectors. These ancient people had experiences that led them to knowledge of and a life with a realm that transcended the physical world in which they lived. That knowledge did not come from their own reasoning, it was not something they discovered. It came about as a Source that existed outside the physical realm intruded itself into their world. "I am the Lord your God, who brought you out of the land of slavery. You shall have no other gods before me" (Duet. 5:6-7).

The reality of this Power that choose them for this relationship cannot be tangibly documented. "No one has ever seen God" (John 1:18). But those encounters with this Spiritual Being had an impact on their lives that was undeniable and of such import that they were recorded, passed down through the generations, and are a treasured legacy. We know that inheritance as the Holy Bible.

Revelation, although not provable through reason, is nevertheless not in conflict with reason. In other words, revelation makes sense!

Revelation opens an additional avenue of growth to us, for it is a continuing phenomenon. It still occurs. The spiritual continues to break into human history. The intrusions come in various ways: through visions, dreams, voices that are not a part of psychotic episodes, whims, intuition, and serendipity, to mention a few. In fact, revelation can operate through any experience available to us. In Chapter Seven we shall present some present-life examples of human encounters with the spiritual realm.

When revelation occurs, the intrusions are always helpful and life-promoting. What is revealed never operates to our detriment, it is always enabling. Whether passed on as historical record or encountered in the here and now, revelation expands our perceptual field. It effects how we are able to see and understand the reality of which life is a part. It operates in the same way that new scientific insight can contribute to our advancement and well being. But scientific advancement that rejects the insights of revelation -- regarding who we are and the purpose of our being -- can result in the destruction of life. Witness the horrors of the nuclear age.

The more we understand, the more powerful we become. We are more in control of our life circumstances, because what we do is less subject to pure happenstance, emotion, or ignorance. Through the understandings which come from revelatory insights, we are able to see a broader arena of reality. That broader perspective remains closed to us if we reject the validity of this spiritual phenomenon. People of faith refer to the phenomenon as "having the eyes of faith." Faith and revelation make it possible to connect with the Spirit of God, who, scripture teaches, is the very definition of Love (1 John 4:8).

This Holy Writ tells us that the Spirit of the Creator is not only with us in our world, but within us as individuals. It says this over and over in many ways. "For thus says the high and lofty

One...'I dwell in the high and holy place, and also with him who is of a contrite and humble spirit'" (Is. 57:15). "Remain in me, and I will remain in you" (John 15:4). "No one has ever seen God; but if we love each other, God lives in us and His love is made complete in us" (1 John 4:12).

People have known this Presence not just from Scriptural testimony, but in a personal way. They have attested their experience with statements like that of Seneca, a Roman philosopher of the first century, "Nothing is void of God; He Himself fills his work." The experience of Merlin Carothers, which is like that of other unnumbered personal testimonies, conveys the genuineness of this Presence.

> Suddenly I heard a deep voice speak directly in my ear. "What -- what did you say?" I whirled around to find no one behind me. There was the voice again: "Tonight you must make a decision for me. If you don't, it will be too late." I shook my head and said automatically: "Why?" (The reply came) "It just will be!" Was I losing my marbles? It was God and he knew me!"[1]

The reality of God's Spirit pervading our humanity has been a part of the human experience through history. Nowhere has it been more beautifully acknowledged than by the ancient psalmist who wrote,

> The Lord is my shepherd, I shall not want.
> He makes me to lie down in green pastures,
> he leads me beside quiet waters,
> he restores my soul.
> He guides me in the paths of righteousness for his name sake (Psalm 23:1-3).

My friend Dan is not in touch with that Presence, because he cannot be open to that which he does not believe exists. His skepticism has prevented his entertaining what the "eyes of faith" would help him to see. Without those "eyes" he cannot see that which would lead him to the treasure. Barring some direct encounter such as Merlin Carothers and others have experienced, Dan at present is not tuned to sense the spiritual aspect of his human nature. He is not positioned to make that connection with the Divine and know the God within him.

To find our way to that personal sense of peace, that Eden place for which we hope, we must be lead by the Being whose garden it is. The journey of faith begins with some conviction that the garden exists and the Gardener is present and anxious to guide us. It continues as the reality of "the Kingdom of God has come upon you" (Luke 11:20) is experienced.

God inside us? We can connect with the spiritual realm now? This is all a part of our human reality? How is this possible? Our task, to which we turn next, is to understand the means by which this can and does happen.

PART IV: WE'RE ALSO CONNECTED TO ETERNITY

> Death and love are two wings which bear men from earth to heaven
>
> Anonymous

CHAPTER 7:
ABOUT LIFE AND DEATH

Jessie (her real name) was a vibrant and attractive divorcee in her mid-fifties who owned and managed a small motel in a rural Virginia town. In her earlier years she worked as a model and retained a physical beauty that matched the attractiveness of her personality. As a result of an accident, she had lost one of her legs, but managed to get around very well with a prosthesis. She was a bright and very interesting woman.

I was Jessie's pastor, but we also considered ourselves to be very good friends. We had spent many hours together in her small apartment behind her office exchanging views on a wide variety of subjects. Therefore it was very upsetting when I learned that she had been hospitalized with some disturbing symptoms. After anxious days of waiting, her doctor told Jessie that she had advanced pancreatic cancer. With the strength of her faith and a healthy sense of self, she faced up to the fact of this terminal condition with fortitude and acceptance.

It was not many months after the diagnosis that Jessie was hospitalized in the final stages of the disease. One afternoon, after we both knew we would soon be separated because of her physical death, we were alone in her room. It was then that I broached the question to her that I so far had not asked. "Jessie," I said, "Are you scared?"

Jessie responded with a broad smile and after a few seconds said, "No, Ernie, I'm not afraid. I'm just damned curious. I can't wait to see what comes next!"

What comes next? Where did Jessie get the resolve that told her death was not an ending, but rather a transition that was going to lead her to something more exciting? How could she face death, which many people fear because they cannot truly view it as anything but the conclusion of life, with such assured confidence that she couldn't wait to see what would come next?

Jessie knew with certainty that we do not die! An understanding of her confidence is worthy of further examination. Hopefully, this exploration will help us to understand our own connection with eternity and to deal with the fear of death with which human beings struggle.

The fear of death seems to be illogical, since most people in the United States believe in an afterlife, according to surveys done in the 1990s. Yet the fear of death is a resident emotion in the psyche of the human race. We live in a psychological state of denial. We use all kinds of language to avoid facing deathly reality: she's departed, he passed away, she has gone to her reward, he kicked the bucket. We do not like to say, "He died," or "She's dead."

Our fear of death, which is the ultimate state of separation from the "known," of being disconnected from what we are consciously aware of, is at the root of an existential anxiety which plagues us. It is a fear of the absolute loss of control over our lives and of the state of "nothingness." It is the primal cause from which our phobias generate.

But if one has such a conviction as my friend Jessie had, the fear is defused. In that state of confidence the passage from this life to what comes next can be a beautiful moment, even though it is steeped in the deep sadness of departure. Following is a vignette that pictures such an experience. This story was related to me by the husband of the woman who died.

Leonard and Ava were in their retirement years. Leonard had been a pastor in one of the main line Protestant churches, she an artist and teacher. Theirs had been fifty-some years of loving relationship with each other, with their children, and with the God that they knew and lived with in daily communion.

His health had been good, she had suffered with some heart problems in the last several years. Although they never dwelled on the thought during their busy and fulfilled life, their faith assured them that we do not die. Their conviction was unwavering.

There was a favorite island vacation spot to which they traveled once a year to spend a month of quiet, pleasant togetherness. While there, in the middle of one night, Ava experienced a severe physical trauma in her chest. She gently woke her husband and in a soft, undisturbed voice said, "Leonard, I'm dying."

"Oh, no," he replied, "No, Ava, I'll call for help."

"No, don't," Ava replied, "It will do no good, Leonard, I know I am going to go. I want to spend these last moments with you." She would not let him leave her.

There were tears in both their eyes as Ava lay there in bed with Leonard sitting up beside her. They exchanged words of love and devotion. Ava told Leonard how much she had enjoyed being his wife and how fulfilled she felt raising their family with him. She told her husband that she would be waiting for him until his time came.

Leonard at the same time was pleading, "No, Ava, don't go, don't leave me. Let me get help, please."

But Ava simply reached up and with ebbing strength kissed Leonard and hung on to him, her arms around his neck. He held her gently in his embrace.

"I love you, dear," she said, "and I will be waiting for you." And with those last words, and the assurance of their life to come, Ava passed through the valley of the shadow of death to claim the hope she always knew would become reality.

SOMETHING OLD, NOT NEW

The confidence of my friends Jessie, and Ava and Leonard is not an isolated conviction. People through eons have expressed a belief in the continuation of life after physical death. Philosophers have expounded on it. Theologians have studied about it and taught what they have learned. Poets have sung about it with their rhymes. Listen to the words of Robert Louis Stevenson,

> He is not dead, that friend, not dead
> But, in the path we mortals tread,
> Gone some few, trifling steps ahead,
> And nearer to the end;
> So that you, too, once past the bend,
> Shall meet again, as face to face, this friend
> You fancy dead.

Then there is the thought, spoken by an anonymous bard, as if it were coming from the beyond.

> Do not stand at my grave and weep;
> I am not there. I do not sleep.
> I am a thousand winds that blow;
> I am the diamond glints on snow.
> I am the sunlight on ripened grain;
> I am the quiet autumn's rain.
> When you awaken in the morning's hush,
> I am the swift uplifting rush of
> Quiet birds in circled flight.
> I am the soft star that shines at night.
> Do not stand at my grave and cry.
> I am not there. I did not die!

The concept of eternal life is graphically portrayed by another anonymous writer in the following allegory with its metaphoric meaning.

> I am standing upon the shore
> A ship at my side spreads her white sails
> to the morning breeze and starts for the blue
> ocean. She is an object of beauty and strength
> and I stand and watch her until, at length,
> she hangs like a speck of white cloud
> just where the sky and sea come down to mingle
> with each other.
> Then someone at my side says,
> "There! She is gone."
> Gone where? Gone from my sight that is
> all. She is just as large in mast and hull and
> spar as she was when she left my side, and
> just as able to bear her load of living
> freight to the place of destination.
> Her diminished size is in me, not in her;
> and at the moment when someone at my side says
> "There! She is gone," there are other eyes
> watching her coming and other voices ready to
> take up the glad shout,
> "There she comes!"

From whence does all this confidence in an eternal existence come? And what is the basis upon which this assurance of a large segment of the human population rests? Much has been written and preached about the belief in and

God's promise of this continuing phase of life. But not much attention has been focused on the reason why life goes on after the experience of physical death.

LIFE HANGS ON

Last summer I became attached to a weed with which I had a running battle. This obstinate piece of flora, that grew up in a seam of my front walk, was persona non grata as far as I was concerned. I pulled it gently out of the seam, attempting to get all the root. A week later it was back in the same spot! So again I carefully extracted the intruder. But again I failed to get it all and, over and over, in a continuing war the little sprout would push up its stem in defiance of my efforts to end its existence.

Now I could have gone to the local Southern States store and gotten a liquid killer that would have done in that offending weed. But somehow I couldn't do that. This little piece of God's creation had won me over with its tenacity to hold on to life and strive toward its fullest potential. And I thought, that's what life does. It hangs in there, holds on, and strives to move forward to achieve its destiny. Life is tough, it's a fighter!

A few winters ago there was a news story about the ordeal of a young couple with a newly born child. They got lost in a once-in-a-century blizzard. They had set off to attend a family affair in another state. While traveling they were engulfed by this huge storm. They lost their way and ended up with their car snowbound in a desolate expanse of wasteland.

They set out on foot to look for help, but fatigue overtook them and they found a small cave in which to huddle. Realizing that no one would find them there, the young father set off for help. After traveling for days and some 20 miles he finally came to a farm. From here he led rescuers back to the cave that sheltered his wife and little baby.

The mother had held her child, huddled in that rock crevice, for three days. She had clung to life herself and protected her child. The father had made an incredible journey on foot in killing conditions. Life hangs in there, holds on, strives to fulfill its destiny. Life is tough, it's a fighter.

BUT WHAT ABOUT DEATH?

Isn't death a killer of life? Doesn't life, with all its toughness and proclivity to hang on and fight for its existence, eventually have to succumb to death? In the face of the Grim Reaper, doesn't life lose its tenacity, must it not loosen its grip and cease its growth? Do we not all have to face the fact that one day our life will end?

The Scriptural answer to those questions is an emphatic NO! Death, the Bible tells us, is not the victor.

> Where, O death, is your victory?
> Where, O death, is your sting?
> (Hosea 13:14)

The Christian faith is grounded in the teaching of Jesus: "I tell you the truth, he who believes has everlasting life" (John

6:47). And then to show that God has power over death, Jesus raised Lazarus, calling him out from his burial tomb (John 11).

Science also is beginning to answer those questions in the negative about the final dominance of death. There is a growing body of research today that indicates that life is bigger than death. That research began to be published years ago with Elizabeth Kubler-Ross' book *On Death and Dying*.

The work by people of science has continued, and been reported in medical journals and scientific meetings. Its findings are available in other popular non-fiction literature: *Life After Life*, and *Reunions: Visionary Encounters With Departed Loved Ones*, by Raymond A. Moody, M.D.; *Closer to the Light*, and *Transformed By the Light*, by Melvin Morse, M.D. *Embraced by the Light* is a first-hand, detailed, and spellbinding account of an after death experience that was had by the author, Betty Eadie.

One, among thousands of such documented experiences, is recounted in the words of a teenager from the projects of East St. Louis.

> I was like nine or ten years old. I don't know how to swim. I was in the peanut pool with my cousins when all of a sudden I was going down. I struggled to breathe and then I just couldn't move any more. Then I thought I was dreaming. I could see myself. It was like I was looking at me. I felt scared. Then I just floated out of my body into a safe place. It was all bright and I felt peaceful.[1]

The investigative work is continuing under the sponsorship of international scientific organizations like The International Association for Near-Death Studies, founded by Dr. Moody and three other scientists. There will be more in depth discussions of these studies in the following chapter.

Then, added to the teaching of scripture and the findings of science, there is the witness of human experience. In a book titled *We Don't Die*, Joel Martin and Patricia Romanowski document the phenomenal story of George Anderson. Anderson is a man gifted with an extraordinary ability to communicate with spirits "on the other side." His gift has been documented through thousands of readings and dozens of scientific tests. Both believers and skeptics have been astonished by the accuracy of his psychic communications. He reveals to people information about events, experiences, and even nicknames, for which the only possible source is a living consciousness.

One of the authors, Joel Martin, was a television personality who heard of Anderson. He got involved with him, he says, with the idea that he was a fraud. But instead of finding evidence of deceit, Martin found such substantiating substance that he not only became a believer, he jointly authored a book to tell others about the extraordinary ability of the man.

Hundreds of people say that Mary and Jesus are calling them to prayer and reconciliation. In our country, the number of reported apparitions or "messages" has exploded. Tens of thousands of pilgrims have converged on a neighborhood in New Jersey, a church in Texas, a hillside in California, and a shrine in Colorado. Many of these were hoping to see Mary or a miracle.

My own work as a chaplain, pastor, and counselor has brought me into personal contact with episodes that shadow another realm. Among anecdotes that I have collected is that of Richie, a six year old boy who was dying from complications stemming from hemophilia.

Richie had some vivid experiences that seemed to comfort him. On one occasion Richie told a hospital chaplain that he had seen Jesus come into his bedroom at night. Another time he saw Jesus, and Jesus had brought Richie's grandfather, who had died, with him. One day Richie told his father that they would have to celebrate his dad's birthday early, because he (Richie) would not be around on the actual date. The family held the party and, as he had predicted, Richie died three days before his dad's birthday.

Then there is the human experience with beings from "the other side" whom we call angels. There are literally hundreds of investigated encounters with these beings which are documented not just in scripture but in such books as *Where Angels Walk: True Stories of Heavenly Visitors*, by Joan Webster Anderson (not related to George Anderson mentioned above) and *Angels among Us,* compiled by the editors of Guideposts magazine.

One such encounter, again among hundreds of documented cases, is that of Kenneth and Suzie Ware. Kenneth was a minister of the Assemblies of God Church serving in the south of France when World War II broke out. Since he was the son of an American soldier, the husband of a Jew, and a supporter of the French resistance, his life was in constant danger.

Eventually Kenneth fled to sanctuary in Switzerland, but found it difficult to provide for his wife and infant son. One morning in September of 1944, they found themselves in their apartment without a penny and in need of food. Suzie decided to pray very specifically for what they needed: five pounds of potatoes, two pounds of flour, apples, pears, a cauliflower, carrots, veal cutlets and some beef. A few hours later a man knocked on their door. He was carrying a basket of groceries. "Mrs. Ware," he said, "I've brought you what you asked for." Suzie protested that there must be some mistake, but the man was adamant. "I've brought you what you asked for," he repeated and began to unload the basket onto the kitchen table. And there on the table Suzie found the exact items she had prayed for, even to the correct brand of flour.

After the man had been thanked and he left the apartment, Kenneth and Suzie stood by the window to watch him depart from the building by the only route available. The man never went by! The couple checked the halls to see if something had happened to him, but he was nowhere to be found.[2]

A DEATH THAT IS FINAL MAKES NO SENSE

Humanity's encounter with a Being, whom many refer to as God, over eons, is recorded in the divinely inspired writings of Scripture. These recorded experiences reveal something of God to those who accept the validity of this writ as holy. They also unfold the purpose behind the creation and God's plan to bring that creation to the fruition intended.

In a nutshell, Scripture teaches that God is the Creator of the cosmos and the parent of all life. God created the world to support his keystone piece, human life. The Creator made people for relationship with the Parent of their life, and consequently with each other. Since this Universal Consciousness has revealed Itself to be loving, this was to be a loving relationship continuing through eternity.

The operating mode of the creation, therefore, is loving relationship functioning in a connected, symbiotic system. Each of its elements is entwined with the others, producing a harmonic blend when existing in healthy community. When in such harmony, civilization moves forward and human life is enhanced. In such a context, death as an ending of life makes no sense. Death is a rational element of this creation only when it is understood as a transition experience in which life transforms from one realm to another. Henry Wadsworth Longfellow explains it with verse,

> There is no death!
> What seems so is transition;
> This life of mortal breath
> Is but a suburb of the life elysian,
> Whose portal we call death.

Healthy, loving parents do not bring children into the world to destroy them. Emotionally stable mothers and fathers, and the societies in which they live, cherish, nurture, and love their children. The desire of good parents is to promote their offspring's well-being, to help them achieve the fullest potential of which they are capable. If healthy human beings hold the life they conceive in such esteem, how much more would a loving God be so inclined toward lives of those the Almighty considers to be daughters and sons?

> The Spirit himself testifies with our spirit that we are God's children. Now if we are children, then we are the heirs -- heirs of God and coheirs with Christ, if indeed we share in his sufferings in order that we may also share in his glory (Romans 8:16-17).

Our Creator then did not give us life to die, but rather brought us forth to live in loving relationship through eternity with Him. If we arrive at any other conclusion we are left with an inglorious and meaningless conclusion to life, a contradiction of that for which we were created. The Christian gospel's message is,

> To life there is no end,
> To death there is no sting;
> The grave is not our final place,
> For in Christ our Savior, we have the resurrection.

THEN WHERE DO WE GO FROM HERE?

If life is a continuing process that has no end, but simply transits from one realm to another, then where is that other place to which we go? Paul, the disciple of Christ, relates his experience with that place for us in his letter to the church at Corinth. He writes,

> I know a man in Christ (referring here to himself) who fourteen years ago was caught up to the third heaven. Whether it was in the body or out of the body I do not know -- God knows. And I know that this man... was caught up to paradise. He heard inexpressible things that man is not permitted to tell (2 Cor. 12:2-4).

Where is heaven, this place of paradise where human beings learn things that cannot be revealed here on earth? If there is to be a life that continues, there must be a milieu in which that existence takes place. To answer such a question we must delve into some spiritual geography, and that will be the subject of the next chapter.

CHAPTER 8:
SOME SPIRITUAL GEOGRAPHY

In the role of Dorothy, the little girl who searched the Land of Oz for the Wizard, Judy Garland sang the thought that all of us have harbored at some time: "If birds fly over the rainbow, why then, oh why can't I?" All of us long for that condition in which the heart knows true contentment and the very soul of us enjoys that peace that transcends all understanding.

In our pleasure seeking, our joining, our consumption, our recreation, our affairs, our charities, our quest for power, our pursuit of wealth, we all search for Wonderland. This is not a new insight, the fact has been written about in all our forms of literature through the ages. It has been put to music and presented on stages. People have explored its many facets ad infinitum. And the search for this heavenly peace goes on in our writings, our songs, our dramas, and our thoughts.

In our need to find this state of well-being, we have erected all kinds of man-made institutions. We have night clubs, golf clubs, civic clubs, social clubs, health clubs, and clubs without end. For our peace of mind we have spent much of our wealth on armies, navies, air forces, nuclear arms, Star Wars technology, and early warning systems. To police ourselves internationally we have invented the League of Nations and the United Nations.

Yes, and we have built churches and temples and mosques. But in our best efforts to capture this prevailing sense of peace, security, and contentment our self-made devices have failed us. There is a restlessness deep in our innards. We experience an existential loneliness, even in the crowds which surround us. We are not sure what it is we need to find.

So if we cannot find it here on earth, our hope is that it will surely lie ahead somewhere in another existence, beyond our present life. "Somewhere over the rainbow bluebirds fly, why then, Oh why can't I?"

Is it that such a condition of contentment and fulfillment cannot exist in our world? Are the conditions of this life simply incapable of supporting that which is necessary for the peace of soul we seek?

Is the present world the "hell" we must endure to earn our way into the "heaven" for which our soul longs? Is our humanity so flawed that we cannot find that which is missing? Must we mark time in anticipation of a life to come? And what of those who may not even be sure that there is such an eternal existence? If there is a heaven, where is it? Is hell a real place, and if so where is that? When do we come into contact with these realities, if realities they are? How do we get there?

To help us with these questions about spiritual geography, we will begin with a true story that unfolded some fifty years ago. It was published in the June 1960 issue of the Christian Herald. It opens some significant insights.

HEAVEN ON EARTH

Hell was here and now for Ernest Gordon, a prisoner of war in a Japanese internment camp in Thailand during World War II. Singapore was captured by the Japanese army and Gordon, along with thousands of other allied defenders, was taken prisoner. All of them were jammed into the Changi POW camp, where sanitation facilities were inadequate, there were no medications for the sick, and the only food was a small daily ration of rice.

From that place many prisoners were transferred to a mosquito-infested and disease ridden camp on the banks of the Kwa Noi river, where the Japanese were building a railway. There, Gordon reported, the Japanese set out to reduce these British captives "to a level lower than any coolie in Asia." The work would have been beyond the strength of even well-bodied men, toiling as they did with baskets to remove dirt in 120 degree heat. Husky men were reduced to skeletons in just weeks.

Illness or the jungle ulcers that developed were no cause for excuse from work. When they fell, men were left to lie in their tracks until they were carried back to camp by fellow prisoners.

They thought that God, if there was a God, did not care about them.

Such conditions brought about deterioration in men's character. The law of the survival of the fittest took over. Those who had been comrades-in-arms stole each other's food, clothing, and whatever else could be used to help them survive. Some betrayed their fellows, seeking favor with the guards by reporting others. In that camp, under these horrendous conditions, prisoners were helping to destroy each other. They were participating in the dismantlement of their own humanity. This was literally Hell!

But something happened to bring about a change. It was not the physical conditions in which they were confined that became different. It was the men in the prison who changed. It came about through the ministrations of two enlisted men, Corporals Miller and Moore. One was a Protestant, the other a Roman Catholic. Gordon reports, "To these two men largely belongs the credit for effecting one of the most wondrous changes I ever witnessed. Not in me alone, but in that entire camp of 3000 men."

Gordon collapsed after two years of such conditions and was given up for "terminal" by the prison medical orderlies that attended him. But the two corporals took him under their care, nursing him and sharing their own food with him. In two and a half months of their care he had his life back. During that time, Gordon learned what these enlisted men were doing.

The two had organized others into small groups. They set examples for relationships in these groups by their own behavior. Miller and Moore shared what they had with the most needy and often gave up their own allotments to others. They organized classes where Christian values were discussed. It started small but spread to include more and more of the prisoners.

Talk led to action, and service groups were generated. Teams of masseurs went to the sick whose muscles had atrophied. Other groups provided different needed services. Men with craft abilities fashioned prostheses for those who had lost limbs. Sandals were made, plants were found from which simple drugs were extracted. Radio technicians devised small radio sets from equipment stolen from their captors. Some risked their lives in communicating with Thai and Chinese Christians outside camp to get food and other supplies. Education groups were formed.

All of this activity focused about the church, which had been erected out of bamboo and jungle grass. Above its altar the prisoners had erected a wooden cross, drawing men's gaze upward toward God and outward toward mankind.

With this recapture of their humanity came an ebbing of their hatred of the Japanese. They began to understand what operated in the lives of their captors to make them behave as they did. With understanding came compassion. The prisoners ceased to see themselves as victims. They learned that the way out of suffering is through it, not avoiding it or denying it.

The change that occurred in them confounded their captors. What was at the root of this dramatic turnabout that enabled men to survive in such devastating conditions? How could men find meaning in such a hell?

Gordon found the answer to these questions when he became aware that the two corporals who started all this had something that the rest of the men had somehow previously missed. "That something," Gordon reports, "was the greatest force on earth -- love. Love that loses life in order to gain it."

Neither of the corporals lived to see the end of the war. Miller died of dysentery on a ship taking him and other prisoners for internment in Japan. Moore was nailed to a cross and left to die by a Japanese officer who hated him for his radiant spirit that refused to break under torture.

The guiding philosophy of their lives was shared with Gordon by Corporal Miller. It was stated in a short poem written by an anonymous poet.

> I sought my soul,
> but my soul I could not see.
> I sought my God,
> but my God eluded me.
> I sought my brother,
> and I found all three.

For the men of that camp on the river Kwa Noi, this kernel of insight turned a "railway of death" into a veritable highway to the abundant life of the Spirit. In the words of Ernest Gordon, "...we'd found life -- life with meaning and purpose, a life strangely sane amid a world gone mad." They had touched heaven on earth in the midst of their personal hell. What does this story tell us about the precincts of heaven and hell?

What the men in this World War II episode experienced seemed a literal hell, which through the amazing power of love was transformed. They found something that helped them preserve life, "strangely sane." What is this "saneness" that was possible in such madness?

A clue to what went on here comes from the New Testament. There Jesus explains, "But if it is by the finger of God that I drive out devils, then be sure the kingdom of God has already come upon you" (Luke 11:20 NEB). In Christian theology God's kingdom -- or the kingdom of heaven which is used interchangeably -- is the realm over which the Almighty rules.

Therefore, this Scripture is teaching that the realm of God's love extends into the present for those who open themselves to it. This understanding is compatible with scripture's teaching that "the kingdom of God does not come with your careful observation, nor will people say, 'Here it is,' or 'There it is,' because the kingdom of God is within you" (Luke 17:20-21).

It was by way of loving relationship that these prisoners entered the heavenly precincts. It is difficult for us to ascertain the borders that mark off boundaries here, for when they gave themselves to each other in loving support, they found themselves a part of a sanity that resided within the madness they were experiencing.

It was as if that sanity already existed and the experience of its reality came when they gave themselves to each other in *agape*, the New Testament commandment to "Love one another"(John 13:34). It was a sanity that found its substance in a certain "meaning and purpose" for life. Once they found that they were through the gates, led by the two corporals who were already residents, they recognized and followed the Sovereign whose domain it was. They were living with God. And they discovered that God had not only been living with them but was a part of them.

Does the experience here show us that we enter the thresholds of Heaven as soon as we commit ourselves fully to the Love that authored life? Perhaps then, Hell is what we experience when we live outside of this realm. This new-found life, Scripture teaches, extends through eternity. There the experience of Heaven is consummated by living in direct association with the Creator. Referring to that time Scripture says, "Now the dwelling of God is with men, and he will live with them. They will be his people, and God himself will be with them and be their God" (Rev. 21:3).

For those prisoners, the hellish conditions of the internment camp did not change. What changed was something inside the men themselves. In the early years of that experience, they had turned into animals. The Hell within them magnified the Hell in which they had to live. With the help of the two corporals, when they tapped the resources of the spiritual part of their humanity, they found their God was already there. They made the Divine connection and they found life. Then the hell around them could not destroy the heaven they had found within themselves. And their captors were absolutely confounded!

ADJUSTING TO A NEW GEOGRAPHY

The ancients knew a God that was Lord of both Heaven and Earth. Although God's presence on earth was believed to reside in the area of their Temple known as the "holy of holies," they conceived Heaven to be God's official place. When God acted it was from "out of Heaven" (Gen. 19:24). That remains the common conception of most people today. Heaven is God's residence and it is located in the sky.

But our present knowledge of space tells us there is really no "sky." The blue that we see when we look toward "heaven" becomes black when examined closely and there is just open space. The canopy that the ancients, and many moderns, thought was there just does not exist. In light of our knowledge, we are forced to revise our ideas about Heaven and where God is.

To help us with this revision, perhaps a good place to start is with the common conception that Heaven is God's place. Heaven is the place where God rules. But as we pursue the matter, we must remember that we are dealing with a spiritual reality and not a physical phenomenon. The ancients had not yet achieved the knowledge of space and the spiritual maturity to completely divorce the physical from the spiritual conceptions of Heaven and Hell.

The ancient Hebrews speculated about various heavens above the earth. Even Paul, the Gospel evangelist of the New Testament, speaks of "the third heaven" (2 Cor. 12:2). But in Christ's return to Heaven he is described as "ascended higher than all the heavens in order to fill the whole universe" (Eph. 4:10). This suggests a transcendence of all space, a moving beyond the physical. Thus a return to another realm, the spiritual, is indicated -- a divorce from the physical notion of heaven as a place existing in time.

If we keep in mind the story of those British prisoners of war, we can use what we saw happening in their situation to form a new perception. Heaven is not a physical place existing in the sky, but the spiritual sphere where God rules. When they discovered that Divine resource within themselves that could overcome the hell in which they were living, they touched base with Heaven. So Heaven may be a condition existing as a part of our own humanity, a state of being with God.

If so, Heaven, then, is a state of being in which we can live or choose not to live. It is that state of mind in which we are open to the Divine Spirit that resides in us. Referring again to Luke's Gospel, "...the kingdom of God is within you."(Luke 17:21)

This then is the mind-set in which we are connected with the spiritual realm out of which the physical was born. Therefore, it is a state of being in which we have already entered the reality of an eternal domain. It is a state in which we have begun to dwell in that sphere from which our spirit, the living essence of our humanity, emanates. It is the frame of mind in which we live under the will of God. It produces a deep contented security experienced by the prodigal who has returned to the comfort and assurances of his home.

THE SPIRITUAL CONNECTION

Listen to the story of a fourteen year old boy as he spoke some years later about his near-death experience, which was the result of an accident.

> I knew I was going to die. But then something happened. It was so immense, so powerful, that I gave up my life to see what it was. I wanted to venture into this experience which started as a drifting into what I could only describe as a long rectangular tunnel of light. But it wasn't just light, it was a protective passage of energy with an intense brightness at the end which I wanted to look into, to touch. ... as I reached the source of the light I could see in. I cannot begin to describe in human terms the feelings I had over what I saw. It was a giant infinite world of calm, and love, and energy, and beauty. It was as though human life was unimportant compared to this. And yet it urged the importance of life at the same time it solicited death as a means to a different and better life. It was all being, all beauty, all meaning for existence. It was all the energy of the universe forever in one place. As I reached my right hand into it, feelings of exhilarating anticipation overwhelmed me. I did not need my body anymore. I wanted to leave it behind, if I hadn't already, and go to my God in this new world.[1]

This account is but one of thousands from the research into near-death experiences mentioned in Chapter Seven. The aim of these studies is not to prove that there is life after life, but they do document human experience in a realm outside that in which our physical body dwells.

These episodes have been proven not to be the result of hallucinations of seriously ill patients, or the result of drug induced fantasies of the mind. The proof has come from valid scientific research reported in respected medical literature.

No one has been able to offer concrete proof that can be physically examined to document the existence of this spiritual sphere. Even though its reality has been supported by overwhelming anecdotal evidence throughout the experience of women and men across the ages, its acceptance is still a matter of faith. The duality of the physical and spiritual is not far-fetched speculation, because it is analogous to a condition in quantum mechanics relative to the wave-particle nature of radiation: a property which is well understood and can be described mathematically, but which is devoid of physical conception.[2]

Consider then the following syllogism. We observe that the physical realm which we call universe exists and human life is a part of that. Scientific understanding and theological conclusion support the premise that there was a beginning episode that brought about what we observe in the physical universe, and it is an axiom of science that for every effect there must be a cause. Then the cause of the inception of the physical realm that we call universe had to be something that existed prior to the physical, a realm outside the natural laws of the universe, a realm which we call the spiritual province.

As noted in Chapter Four, Stephen Hawking has written, "It would be very difficult to explain why the universe should have begun this way (the Big Bang theory), except as an act of a God who intended to create beings like us."[3] And from there we can turn to Paul Huber's explanation, "Our creation story starts at the first, split second of time, when God took a bit of his spiritual power and used it for the genesis of the transformation process"[4]

Thus the physical realm can be understood as being born out of the power of the spiritual sphere. The Creator is the Conscious Force that acted from that spiritual realm to author life and what we experience as physical reality. Although we belong to that physical domain there is an aspect of our humanity that is not restricted to it. We are made in the image of that Conscious Force that exists beyond the physical. We can connect with the Divine, and with each other in ways that cannot be explained by the natural laws of the physical world.

WE ARE NOT APES

There are unnumbered examples of a communication link that operates within the reality of our human experience, although we just do not understand its mechanics. Dr. Melvin Morse, whose books were referred to in the Chapter Seven, recounts his personal experience with that reality. This is his story.

> Months before my father died, he sat down in my living room and told me that he was going to die soon.

> Most of my father's intestines had been surgically removed ten years earlier for cancer of the colon, and he had had triple bypass surgery. On top of that he refused to take his heart medicine since it left him impotent ...The night he died, I was exhausted from work and had turned off my telephone. As I dozed off, I saw my father. "Melvin, call your answering service," he said, "I have something to tell you. I called and was told to contact my mother immediately. She told me that he had died."[5]

This episode is not some weird anomaly. A Swiss study, referred to by Morse, scientifically documents that parents of children who die of crib death often have premonitions of the event. In my own book *Living With God in Loss*, in a chapter titled "But how are we connected?" I have documented similar cases of communication that go beyond what natural law can explain."[6]

Teresa Apgar of Richmond, Virginia was influenced by some unexplained premonition to turn away from her normal route home. By doing so she saved a man from a burning truck. A helicopter pilot in Vietnam responded to a sudden, overpowering urge and turned off course to find and rescue a seriously wounded officer. Armando Valladares tells of a Presence that he was very much aware of that made it possible for him to survive twenty-two years of tortuous political imprisonment.

There is an aspect of our human nature, something we do not see but can feel, that goes beyond the physical and has the capability to connect with a reality outside the sphere of natural law.

Ancient wisdom was aware of that aspect of our nature. From the insight of revelation, the Hebrew people ascribed this capability to the Creator of life: "The Lord who stretches out the heavens, who lays the foundation of the earth and *who forms the spirit of man within him...*" (Zech. 12:1, Italics mine). And again, "And the Lord formed man of the dust of the ground, and breathed into his nostrils the breath of life; and man became a living soul" (Gen. 2:7).

It is this spiritual aspect that women and men have always seen as defining our humanity, differentiating our life from all other living forms. It is what makes us different from the apes. Seneca wrote, "The soul alone renders us noble." And that recognition has continued through the ages as this part of our human make-up has been recognized and validated.

Samuel Taylor Coleridge wrote, "Either we have an immortal soul, or we have not. If we have not we are beasts; the first and wisest of the beasts it may be, but still beasts..." He then goes on to note that there are acknowledged differences between us and the beasts and concludes, "'therefore, me thinks, it must be the soul within us that makes the difference."

Harold Bruce Hunting identifies this part of our nature as the core of our constitution: "Man," he writes, "does not have a soul, he is one." And Gottfried Wilhelm von Liebnitz sees this part of us as the connection with the entire cosmos: "The soul," he proclaims, "is the mirror of the indestructible universe."

How real is this spiritual part of what we are? Is it more than just a matter of conjecture, based on undefined feelings we have that we conveniently explain by concocting such an explanation? St. Augustine saw it as a part of us that connects the physical body with the power that makes the body alive, giving us life. As noted previously, he taught: "The life whereby we are joined unto the body is called the soul."

Some very recent research gives credence to this theological explanation. It was conducted by Dr. Melvin Morse and other researchers, and reported in Morse's book *Closer to the Light*. Morse says that this research, which has been reported in medical meetings and journals, has changed his life, including his views on medicine, the way he sees society, and even the way he interacts with his family. He reports,

Our research brought together new and preexisting information that revealed a genetically imprinted circuit in the brain that can generate near-death experience. The existence of that area has caused me to include the concept of the soul in my medical thinking. Why? The simplest, most logical way to explain our current knowledge of man's consciousness is the hypothesis that there is actually a soul within each of us, independent of brain tissue...

I have documented that we have an area in the brain, the right temporal lobe, described by some researchers as the seat of the soul. It is connected to the hippocampus, which serves as the brain's master control... (which) has been called "the man in the machine" by some neurologists.

I once heard a minister preach that a small piece of God is in each and every one of us. I thought to myself: "God is in everyone of us, and the ability to perceive God is located in the right temporal lobe, within the Sylvian fissure."[7]

And this actual presence of God seems to make a difference in the way we can function. This ability we have to be in touch with the spiritual realm gives us a powerful control over our living. That power has been observed, but never before recent decades has it been scientifically documented.

Norman Vincent Peale wrote of it over forty years ago in a classic work, *The Power of Positive Thinking*. In that book he proclaimed and documented through anecdotal evidence the fact that we can influence our own life circumstances, both physically and psychologically, through the power of our mind. Since that time a whole new field of medicine has developed called psychoneuroimmunology, a long word that refers to the study of the interconnection of the mind, the brain, and the immune system. The research that is being done in this field is providing scientific verification for what Peale observed and reported. There is a connection between the mind, the brain, and the immune system of the body. They function in an interrelated manner. Consider the following evidence.

It is a fact that if an anesthesiologist tells a person she/he will get well soon, that person will leave the hospital, on the average, two days sooner than patients in a control group who were not told that. Studies have also shown the value of talking to patients concerning postoperative pain and the healing process. These patients, too, leave the hospital, on average, two days sooner than patients in a control group who do not have such communication. It is also a fact that insurance agents who have been identified as having positive mental outlooks sell ten percent more policies than the average representative working for the company.

This positive attitude and its effects on healing is not simply the operation of what psychologists label "denial," a false idea that we are immortal and nothing can really hurt us. The positive attitudes documented seem to have a link to the spiritual realities of our human nature. Dr. Isaac Djerassi of Philadelphia was quoted as saying, "We now have convincing evidence that the right mental attitude can help your immune system function more effectively. I have treated more than ten thousand people with cancer during the past thirty-three years; the people with faith are always the best fighters."[8]

This link between faith and our functioning as human beings is the subject of Dr. Bernie S. Segal's book *Love, Medicine, and Miracles*. In his book he indicates that one of the most important sources of our strength is this connection we have with God and nature. Our ability to be in loving relationship, his clinical experience tells him, is a powerful incentive to healing. "I am convinced," he writes, "that unconditional love is the most powerful known stimulant to the immune system. If I told patients to raise their blood levels of immune globulins or killer T cells, no one would know how. But if I can teach them to love themselves and others fully, the same changes happen automatically. The truth is: love heals."[9]

CHILDREN OF THE LIGHT

As we have moved through this chapter, I hope that we have seen more clearly the reality of two spheres of life, the physical and the spiritual. Both of them are important in understanding who we are, where we have come from, and where we have evidence to believe we are going.

Those who have had near-death experiences and feel that they have touched this spiritual world associate it with "light." Scripture often speaks of light when it teaches about God's domain. "What is the way to the abode of light," it asks (Job 38:19). The psalmist sings, "Blessed are those... who walk in the light of your presence, O Lord" (Ps. 89:15). The prophet extends comfort to those in distress; "The people walking in darkness have seen a great light; on those living in the land of the shadow of death a light has dawned" (Isa. 9:2). And the New Testament speaking of God's incarnation says, "The true light that gives light to every man was coming into the world" (John 1:9).

So in our quest to understand life more fully, to know who we are, whence we came, and where we are going, perhaps we have discovered that we are "children of the light." Perhaps we have been born out of a spiritual world, a connection to which is planted deep within us in that right temporal lobe. If so then that is our home, the place from which our life emanates, and the place to which we will return when our earthly journey is finished.

Perhaps our understanding can now go even further than that: Is it that we are of the spirit, made in the Creator's image (Gen. 1:26), and in our present time housed in the physical realm? Is the essence of our humanity not the body which houses our being at the moment, but the soul within us which finds temporary abode in a physique through which we operate in a physical reality? Our body is not "us," it is simply the residence where the "I" which is me currently lives.

Perhaps it is this essence of our humanity, the soul, with which we have lost touch. Is it this loss that powers the quest for inner peace, the void that we keep trying to fill with things, and recreational diversions, and other pursuits? Does our human dilemma lie in the fact that we have cast aside the spiritual component of our nature and tried to ignore it in an attempt to build a pseudo-self that can be the god of its own life?

Can our problem be that this false being we have contrived thinks it can be the "master" of all it surveys, setting its own purposes and goals for life, without connection to anything but its own needs and appetites? And if so, have we not lost touch with that which defines what we are, which sets us off from all other created life, and which makes us human?

And if all these "perhapses" are true, would they not explain the deep loneliness that inhabits our hearts, because we have alienated ourselves from the Source of life, from each other, and from the whole creation of which we are a part? Would they not account for the powerful combination of need and anxiety which grips us: the need for that inner peace which we cannot find and the anxiety that grows out of our sense of absolute aloneness?

To maintain the fiction of our own independence and power, we have ignored our finitude, we have denied our vulnerability, and we have forgotten our fealty to the Parent that gave us life. And in so doing, we have lost touch with the essence of who we are, the place from which our life came, the reason we are here, and the place to which we are called to return.

We have lost, or obliterated, the connection with a reality that goes beyond the present and would associate us with a realm out of which our life was spawned. We have blinded ourselves by the disregard of this unseen aspect of our humanity, so that our vision is too narrow. We see only the physical, the day to day, the trivial, the limited. When the meaning of our life comes from such a restricted view, the only conclusion we can draw is: all that matters is "now," we ourselves are the architects of that moment, and death will bring it all to an end.

To turn our situation around, we must find and renew that connection to the Divine we have lost. We are children of the Light. We are claimed by that Parent from whom our life emanates. As St. Augustine taught, "Thou movest us to delight in praising Thee; for Thou hast formed us for Thyself, *and our hearts are restless until they find rest in Thee*" (Italics mine).

The peace that humanity searches for, the soul-deep sense of well-being that each of us seeks, the assurance we need that life is an eternal experience, all depend on our re-connection with the Source of our life. In the final section of the book we will look at resolving our self-made dilemma.

PART V:
SO WE CAN GET OUT OF THE MESS

> Heaven is not reached in a single bound;
> But we build the ladder by which we rise
> From lowly earth to vaulted skies,
> And we mount to its summit round by round.
>
> John Gilbert Holland

CHAPTER 9: REMAKING THE CONNECTION

We have been examining a paradox women and men face with regard to their designed place in the Creator's eternal plan. It evolves from the fact that humanity needs to recapture a lost part of itself -- a part that can admit to its own dependence and vulnerability. Seeking to find that illusive inner peace that has not been achieved, humanity also remains forever careful about any relationship with an "Other" whose intimacy and intensity are powerful -- strong enough to cause the recall of that archaic bond within which shalom was first experienced. Thus humanity keeps itself rigidly separate, tightly under control, so as not to lose the fabricated illusion of its own power and independence. And in doing so the connection needed with the Source of the very peace for which the soul searches is interrupted.

In other words, we are our own worst enemy! By our own stubborn desire for autonomy and sovereignty, we block our way to the fullness of life that we so desperately seek -- that which "having and getting" has not accomplished for us.

To be the persons we were created to be, to be what I will call *Real,* we must resolve that paradox. We must learn to be authentic. What does this kind of person look like?

WHAT "REAL" LOOKS LIKE

We have all seen "Real", it marks the lives of those who have found Eden. We have seen it in the life of Mother Teresa, who through the decades of the twentieth century has lived in loving relationship with her God and with God's creation. This woman has become an international celebrity, not because it was her desire, but because her love is so pure and real that it captures the attention and respect of all who observe it.

We have seen "Real" in the lives of people like William Borden, heir to the Borden Dairy estate. When, on a trip that his parents gave him as a high school graduation gift, he saw the suffering of the world's hurting people. He wrote home saying, "I'm going to give my life to prepare for the mission field." He did that and on his way to serve in China, he contracted cerebral meningitis in Egypt and died. After his death it was discovered that he had written three words in the back of his Bible: No Reserves, No Retreats, No Regrets.

We have seen "Real" in Maximilian Kolbe, a Polish monk, who in a German concentration camp during World War II volunteered to be executed in place of another man. The other man had cried out when his number was called, "My poor wife! My poor children! What will they do?"

We have seen "Real" in the myriad of media reports of people who put themselves at risk, or make personal sacrifices on behalf of strangers who are in peril or trauma – witness the heroes of 9/11. We have seen Real in the lives of those quiet saints, who in their ordinary routines, as a matter of course, share what they have, give of themselves in service, feel for their neighbors, forgive when they are wronged, and never seek payment or recognition for what they do.

We have seen the fundamental character of "Real", it is love. What does it look like in the neighborhood in which we live? Susan showed it to those of us who knew her.

Susan (her real name) was a Christian friend of mine. And not only mine; Susan was a friend to everyone in her county. Everyone knew and loved Susan. She was a small lady with a big heart. She spoke with a tiny voice that to hear you had to listen carefully. The voice came out of lips that always seemed to smile. When I first met her she had retired and lived in a small, unpretentious house. Her retirement days continued to be filled with what her days had always held: finding people in need and helping them.

Susan was a pack rat, she would never allow you to throw anything away. Her back porch and garage were like a warehouse. Her vocation and avocation were the same: matching what she had with people who had need of stuff she collected. She moved quietly, without fanfare into the lives of people, loving them with her gentle caring.

Susan died some years back and all of us who knew her lost a precious gift. Out of her small body radiated a serenity that was a reflection of the deep inner peace that reigned inside her. No one doubted that she walked in harmony with the creation of which she was part. Susan did not have much in the way of earthly treasure, but she claimed a wealth that kings could only envy. Her life was blessed, because it was a blessing to others. Susan was a personification of the promise: "Blessed are the meek, for they shall inherit the earth" (Matthew 5:5).

Susan was a portrait of "authentic".

LOOKING OUTWARD

This kind of loving has a unique perspective; it looks outward to others, rather than focusing inward on self. It is the necessary stance for connection. When our focus is inward, we see and feel only personal needs and appetites. And the satisfaction of these becomes our preoccupation. When these take complete precedence, our motives become self-centered and narrow. It is not possible from this position to see beyond our own limited rationality, to grasp a larger, more functional, more beautiful design whose grandeur and power enhances all who are a part of it.

Looking inward allows only a confined perspective. Looking inward upon self prevents our achieving a sense of "oneness with" that comes from investing ourselves in each other, sharing a unity that exists in the bond of our common humanity. Focusing inward obliterates our vision of others, their needs, desires, aspirations, worthiness, and integrity as individuals. It blocks our connection with the Divine. In that state we lose sight of family and community and eternity.

On the other hand, looking outward from self enables us to see that all of us are of the same substance, linked by life circumstances in a common enterprise. Looking outward promotes a sense of common identity, because though separate and individual, we can see we are part of the same whole. We grasp the larger picture. We apprehend an eternal creation.

Looking outward from self is the only stance from which we can achieve genuine agape relationship, because love looks outward from self to see and feel as "other" sees and feels. To love is to experience in resonance with each other. From that stance the "oneness" of family, community, and the world are a natural consequence.

When we look outward we encompass a broader horizon. We see more things. We see new things. Naaman was an ancient man of great power who came to a whole new perspective on life after an encounter with a prophet of Israel.

Naaman was an Aramean who was the commander of the army of the king of Aram. But Naaman had a serious health problem. He had been afflicted with leprosy. Through the good offices of a Jewish slave girl who worked in his household, Naaman, with his whole entourage, went to Elisha seeking a cure for his dread disease. When the commander came to his door, the prophet of Israel sent word to him through a servant to wash seven times in the river Jordan and he would be cured. Naaman, who had tremendous authority, was used to great respect. So he was furious at the lack of personal attention and the instructions he had been given.

The man had a preconceived idea as to how this whole thing should unfold and, from his perspective, it was not going that way. He angrily left the prophet's house saying, "I thought he would surely come out to me and stand and call on the name of the Lord his God, wave a hand over me and cure me of my leprosy" (2 Kings 5:11). Naaman's focus was inward on self and he could not accept events that did not agree with his conceptions.

But Naaman's servants prevailed upon him to do this little thing that had been suggested. So the great man went to the river and he did as he had been instructed. After he bathed seven times in the Jordan his flesh was restored, he was cleansed of his disease, and his skin became like that of a young boy.

As you may well understand, after that Naaman's whole perception changed. He now realized that there were things beyond his ken that he had not been able to see before. He said, "Now I know that there is no other God in all the world except in Israel" (2 Kings 5:1-15).

When we are able to look outward, it is possible to perceive realities to which we otherwise close ourselves. The evidence of the spiritual realm is all about us. There are miraculous medical cures, documented to the extent that mere chance is ruled out.

There is personal testimony recorded concerning guidance, rescue, and other miraculous acts that are so numerous they go beyond coincidence. There are episodes of other personal contact with a realm whose effects on our life are simply mysterious to us.

But outside these stupendous events where the spiritual realm breaks into human history through mechanics that we do not understand, there are miracles that occur every day through the ordinary processes of life. People who are in some kind of desperate need are brought into contact with someone who can help them.

Insights are opened concerning problems we must solve or dilemmas we face. They come through a chance word someone speaks to us, or a few sentences we read in something we just picked up by chance. People pray for help and because they sincerely believe in the power of prayer they are moved in directions that they previously had not considered. People face enormous tragedy and somewhere within them they find a strength, not only to endure but to climb up and go on.

There is a power and a guidance that is available, if we have the vision to recognize it, that enables us to do what we cannot do on our own. Everyday this power acts through what I call these *miracles of the ordinary*, because they come through the day to day channels of our living. And they can happen to all of us if we simply learn to recognize and acknowledge them. They are part of the mysterious process by which we are connected to the spiritual realm.

This is the reality of something about which Jesus taught when he told his disciples, "Unless I go away the Counselor will not come to you; but if I go, I will send him to you" (John 16:7). This is the reality of the divine promise, "And surely I am with you always, to the very end of the age" (Mat. 28:20). This reality can only be recognized when we are looking outward, beyond the focus of our own finite constitution and rationality. This is the reality of connection.

There is a therapy in this outward focus, as Carlo Carretto points out in his little book on suffering *Why, O Lord?* In discussing how to handle the traumatic episodes of life he observes,

> Then, all things being equal, in time of suffering the easiest way to allay suffering... is to get out of myself, visit someone who is suffering worse than I am, do something to remind me of the suffering of the world, set my heart in order if I feel a residual dislike of someone, write a check for the world's poorest mission... In other words, perform an act of love that requires patience and honesty.[1]

REACHING OUT TO TOUCH

Looking outward involves reaching outward. Being able to touch each other and share at the gut level of our humanity, where our honest feelings lie, is the basis for being authentic. The sharing of touch is one of the greatest elixirs in life: a hand on hand, the warm embrace of hug, stroke of cheek, gentle pat of shoulder, caress. We savor its uplifting, reassuring pleasure, but we have lost sight of its magnificence.

All of us have known its effect, but we do not fully credit its value and importance. To touch is to speak, but in silent voice; it is to impart feeling with an impact that is different from even the most tender, sincere words. To be touched is to experience a sensation of joining with, but it also sends a spiritual message of unity that goes to the inner loneliness of our human condition.

Touching is a gift, available for exchange. It is a preciousness we can give and receive. Things loved are touched, often worn to a soft finish by our handling. Touch says, "I'm with you, whatever your condition may be, I will share it with you." It conveys the message, "I care; you are not alone." It lifts us when blue, it joins us in our joys. It is a gesture of healing, for it says, ultimately, "I love you." And love, as we discovered earlier in this book, heals.

There is a therapeutic quality to touch. In researching his book *Healing and the Mind*, print and broadcast journalist Bill Moyers found the importance of touch cropping up as a recurring theme. He reports that from babies to older adults, human beings mysteriously experience healing benefits from being massaged. Studies have shown that infants who are touched frequently grow and develop better than those who are not. When a doctor takes time to hold a patient's hand it aids the healing process.

Touch, then, is not simply one dimensional; it is not just a physical experience. There is the emotional element of touch in which spirit embraces and speaks with spirit: the "Rocky Mountain High" that John Denver extols in song; soil sieved caringly through the calloused fingers of a farmer; the harmonic chords of symphony; poet thoughts that sing through rhymed verse; the magnificence of nature's grandeur; the prayers of the ancient psalmists who express every feeling of our human condition. No, hands are not the only instrument of touch; we touch and are touched by the things of heart, mind, and soul.

What is this mystery about touch that harbors dimensions of which we have no understanding? Touch reaches into and out of that spiritual realm that exists beyond the physical. Listen to this story that illustrates the point.

There was a woman who had a problem with her menstrual cycle. She could not stop the bleeding, which had gone on for twelve years. She was in a crowd of people who had surrounded Jesus of Nazareth as he was moving about. She thought, "If I only could touch his cloak, I will be healed." So she reached out as he passed by and touched the edge of his garment. Jesus felt that touch and through it something mystical happened. The woman was healed (Matthew 9:20-22).

I have previously referred to the studies of Dr. Melvin Morse with people who have had near death experiences and his scientific findings concerning those who have been *Transformed by the Light*.

The mystic qualities of touch have been recognized for a long time, growing out of experiences such as Jacob's report of being touched by God (Gen. 32:25-30), Isaiah's account of being cleansed by touch (Isa. 6:7), and the crowds who pressed in upon Jesus that they might touch him to be healed (Luke.

6:19). The miraculous acts of Jesus often involved touching (Matthew 8:3, 15; 14:36). An ancient ritual of the church is the laying on of hands, by which the authority and power of office are transmitted.

Recall also those special moments of your life when a sight, an act, a ceremony, a thought, a word, a song, an embrace, a prayer touched you emotionally. There is a mystery about touch; it reaches into and out of the spiritual.

To tap into this mystery it is necessary to be open to its possibilities. And because of our alienation we have grown out of touch. We have lost that genuine part of us because we have ignored, and often even denied, the aspect of our humanity that has the capacity to connect with the spiritual realities of life.

The genetic mechanism is there -- identified through rigorous scientific investigation as occurring in the Sylvian fissure of the right temporal lobe of the brain, but we fail to allow ourselves to be open to its possibilities. Someone has said that God cannot fill what is not open to him. In our arrogant belief that we can be the god of our own life, we have drifted away from contact with the spiritual and lost touch with that which is a functional part of the real us.

FORGIVENESS THROUGH COMPASSION

Looking outward involves reconciliation. It is often difficult for us to forgive. As Carretto reminds us in his little book referred to in chapter 4, "The fact of the matter is that loving is difficult. And so is forgiving, truly forgiving."[2]

When we are the innocent victim of a deep hurt inflicted by someone to whom we have given our friendship and love, someone to whom we have opened our heart, we get angry. And it is not easy for us to discharge the intense feelings we experience as the injury fires our emotions. To release these charged feelings, our tendency is to want to strike back or lash out at those who have wounded us. And if we don't take overt action, we at least feel justified in cloaking ourselves in a resentful distancing that communicates our hurt and anger.

Many of us might think it not unnatural to act in such a way, and do so. But forgiveness is an important quality of the love connection. Recall the old adage, "To err is human, to forgive Divine." If we are unable to forgive, we are unable to truly love in the way agape has been defined.

But how can we ignore the fire that is generated by deep hurt and go on as if it had not happened? Is it humanly possible to quell the charged emotions that are a part of our human mechanism? If we are centered inward on self and unwilling to focus outward, then the answer is, "No, it is probably not possible."

For as we focus inward we maintain the thoughts surrounding our hurt and the feelings that accompany that injury to our ego. Feelings follow thoughts. That is, our emotions are generated from the thoughts that are active in our mind. We see danger, think "I may be hurt," and we feel fright. So if we maintain an inward focus that does not relinquish the thoughts of hurt we suffered, we also maintain the feelings of resentment.

And we will be unable to release them. We will be unable to forgive.

    Then what is our alternative? How can we honestly let go of the hurt and bring about the reconciliation that will heal our self and the relationship? The answer lies in the direction of our view. If we are willing to look outward to those who have violated our friendship and love, we can seek to understand their situation.

    What was going on in their lives that would have prompted such behavior toward me? What experiences have they had that caused them to injure the honest affection I offered to them? Why are they so broken that they cannot receive and return the love that I sincerely would share with them?

    When we can focus on the brokenness that brought about the injury to our innocence, we have a whole new set of thoughts to occupy our thinking. We open ourselves to understand what is behind the meanness, the narrowness, the pettiness, the jealousy, the self-centeredness, the personal hurt, the insecurity, the emotional poverty, or whatever else may have been at the root of the hurt that was inflicted on us. When we can find that brokenness, we can then look on it with compassion.

Compassion is an antidote for hurt and anger. When we can look outward, with compassion, we can forgive. That is not to say that we will experience the closeness we had once hoped for in a relationship. The corresponding willingness of the other person to respond in love would also affect that. But our forgiveness can lead to reconciliation and the healing that reconciliation can bring to each party who is open to it.

A PARADIGM FOR PARDON

One of the most poignant illustrations of forgiveness was depicted by Jesus in a parable that he used with some Pharisees and teachers. These religious leaders of their day did not understand that forgiveness is an essential aspect of love and healing. They muttered against Jesus for associating with those whom they considered to be unforgivable sinners. They criticized him to the crowds that gathered around Jesus, saying, "This man welcomes sinners and eats with them" (Luke 15:2).

In reply Jesus told this story. There was a man who had two sons. The younger son came to him asking for his share of the family estate so that he might go off and make his own way in the world. The father granted the request, and the lad set off for a distant land. There he squandered his inheritance in reckless fashion until it was entirely gone. A famine then struck this country and the boy had to hire himself out to a farmer who had him slopping his pigs. The young man was so hungry that he thought about eating the pods he was feeding to the pigs.

But he finally came to his senses, thinking, "How many of my father's men have food to spare and I sit here starving. I will return to my home and confess my wrongdoing. I will not ask to be recognized as a son, for I am not worthy of that, but I will request that my father simply make me as one of his hired men." So he set off for his father's house.

But while he was still a long way off, his father saw him and was filled with compassion. He ran to his son, threw his arms around him, and kissed him. The son confessed his unworthiness. But his father called on servants to bring a new robe and sandals for him. He ordered a ring for his finger and the killing of a calf for a feast. And deep from within his heart the father expressed his joy, saying, "Let's have a feast and celebrate. For this son of mine was dead and is alive again; he was lost and is found" (Luke 15:11-24).

Forgiveness is an essential element of agape. It is motivated by compassionate love. This empathy is born out of a heart that can be in resonance with another. It can only come from a perspective that looks outward from self - the perspective of those who are "Real".

LIVING TOGETHER IN COMMUNITY

Being fully connected with the whole creation of which we are a part puts us in a balance which is like that which we find in a healthy ecological system. The soil, water, sunlight, plant life, animals, and human life actually become a part of each other. There is a cyclical interconnectedness that when properly in balance promotes the well-being of the entire system, each part contributing to and being contributed to by each element - a field dynamic.

Being together in loving association is like that. A balanced ecological system can serve as an analog for agape relationship. People who are living in healthy community are integrated emotionally and function together in a balanced, mutually supportive unit. The healthy family is such an entity. The community of which Scott Peck writes in *The Different Drum,* mentioned in chapter 2, describes this way of being together. The well-being of all who live in such spiritual union, as well as the group life as a whole, is promoted.

This is not to say that in this kind of association all grief, strife and sadness are eliminated, for these things are a reality of honest togetherness. But in agape relationship there is present and functional the mutual bond of a common humanity, in synchrony with the creation of which it is part, that is able to work its way through all the exigencies of living together.

And this sense of community does not just apply in the physical realm of life. When Jesus taught that the kingdom of God "has come to you," and that "the kingdom of God is within you," he was alluding to this sense of community. When we are in loving relationship with God, the eternal system, and each other, we are in community with the spiritual realm. It is in this sense that the encounter with the Creator's domain begins for us in the here and now. In our present life on earth, we begin our experience of heaven through the mechanism of community. But achieving the emotional integration which produces such a bond of spiritual unity requires a willingness to be honest with ourselves and be open to God and each other.

In dealing with each other, we must be secure enough about who we are to allow others to share our selfhood. We must each be able to understand how life may look through the eyes of the other. We must be confident enough in our own legitimacy and authenticity to be our real self with each other - to be anxious, happy, afraid, depressed, to make mistakes, to express our deepest feelings - even though at times this may cause us hurt when someone treats our honesty in an unloving way. This is a risk that love involves.

And in like manner, we must risk with God. First, to accept that the Creator is there and in control of everything. Then we must be willing to bet our life on God's love. We must risk that the promises will be kept. This requires the trust of faith, for God does not reveal the Divine Self directly. "Now faith is being sure of what we hope for and certain of what we do not see" (Heb. 11:1).

C.S. Lewis writes of this risk, but also the consequence of not taking it, in a piece that was quoted in the magazine *Alive Now!*

> To love at all is to be vulnerable. Love anything and your heart will certainly be wrung and possibly be broken. If you want to make sure of keeping it intact, you must give your heart to no one, not even an animal. Wrap it carefully round with hobbies and little luxuries; avoid all entanglements; lock it up safe in the casket or coffin of your selfishness. But in that casket -- safe, dark, motionless, airless -- it will change. It will not be broken; it will become unbreakable, impenetrable, irredeemable. The alternative to tragedy, or at least to the risk of tragedy, is damnation. The only place outside heaven where you can be perfectly safe from all the dangers and perturbations of love is hell.[3]

But in this risk that we take through agape, we each make an investment in the other, we become a part of each other, and God's presence becomes a reality to us. "They will be my people and I will be their God"(Jer.31:33). Together we become transformed, a new thing, a greater entity, a pair, a family, a community, a world citizen, a participant in the heavenly realm. We become more powerful, more effective than any of us can be individually. We become a larger life form, like the myxotricha paradoxa described in Chapter Three, an organism which is a community of individual life forms.

Love is a connector that brings us together; supporting our ability to function in real union and become something grander than any of us could be as individuals. It enables us to achieve the fullness of our humanity and become what we were created to be!

AN ANCIENT AND A MODERN EXAMPLE

The epitome of this kind of relationship is beautifully expressed in the words of Ruth, a Moabite woman who became the daughter-in-law of a Hebrew mother, Naomi. Naomi had moved to the land of the Moabites with her husband and two sons because of a famine in their homeland. The two sons married Moabite women. Naomi's husband died, and after about ten years the sons also died. Naomi then decided to return to her home in Bethlehem and urged her two daughters-in-law to remain in their own land and remarry. But such was the love of

Ruth for Naomi that she entreated her mother-in-law to allow her to go with her, saying,

> Don't urge me to leave you or turn back from you. Where you go I will go, and where you stay I will stay. Your people will be my people and your God my God. Where you die I will die, and there I will be buried. May the Lord deal with me, be it ever so severely, if anything but death separates you and me (Ruth 1:16-17).

A modern demonstration of this kind of love connection was witnessed by Marwann Binni, a thirty-two-year-old United States Marine staff sergeant. Sergeant Binni was among the first American troops to enter the town of Baidoa in Somalia in December 1992.

The people of Somalia were living in a state of anarchy at this time because of the absence of a central government. There had been a severe food shortage for months and people were dying by the thousands. When the troops entered the town with relief supplies the human devastation was so great that it made some of the soldiers weep. One skinny little boy in the crowd of hungry people that had come out to welcome the troops caught Sergeant Binni's attention with a charming smile. Binni reached out and offered the hungry boy a piece of candy. "You know what?" Binni said. "This kills me. He smiles, he takes the candy, and he gives it to someone else. He shares it!"

That is what agape looks like in real life.

THE SURRENDER OF WILL

To achieve that outward focus we have been discussing, we must find the authentic person who lives within each of us. We cannot be authentic in our relations with things outside us until we are able to be genuine with our self. That is, we must admit to and be comfortable with who we are: I am a child of God, I am loved and wanted. I am dependent upon the Creator who gave me life. I am limited in what I can do and vulnerable to forces beyond my control. We must give up the Great Lie that we have tried to maintain: that we can be our own god, the master of the purpose for life, and the judge of how life should unfold.

And this surrender to reality must be more than an intellectual acquiescence. It must be more than lip service to an idea that reason acknowledges, but to which the heart refuses to pay heed. It must have the power of emotional commitment, rising within us from that place where our surest beliefs are born. It must be an affirmation that we sincerely make.

It is necessary to honestly face the fact that we have not been genuinely who we were created to be. And we must admit that the deception started with deceiving our self. Such honesty opens us to the fact of our place in the creation and the reality of our connection to all its aspects. Such awareness brings us to the fullness of our potential for relationship. But it takes courage to face our self in this way.

So in this transformation we must become as the young child is: children are honest; they do not try to turn their fantasies into reality; they acknowledge their dependence; they accept the mysteries of life that they do not understand, for they place full trust and confidence in those who express love for them; they open themselves whole-heartedly to love; they acknowledge their place in the scheme of things; they admit to their childhood. Scripture puts it this way,

> I tell you the truth, unless you change and become like little children, you will never enter the kingdom of heaven. Therefore, whoever humbles himself like this child is the greatest in the kingdom of heaven (Matthew 18:3-4).

From the stance of the child, and only from that stance, we can turn to the Parent who is the source of our life. If we are not gods, then we can seek that Universal Consciousness which brought life into being and the system that supports life. The reality of that Infinite Power and the spiritual realm out of which that Power acts has already been discussed in prior chapters.

This Creator is a revealing God, for through the ages of human history this Lord has been visible as the Parent of life and the creation, the Incarnate Son who taught and modeled Divine Love, and the resident Spirit whose presence abides and acts in the world. That Creator authored life out of love, for through the prophet spokesperson the message has come, "I have loved you with an everlasting love; I have drawn you with loving kindness" (Jer. 31:3).

LIVING WITH AN ABIDING PRESENCE

When we admit to who we really are and from whence we have come, we find we are not alone, not ever. There is a sheltering Love, a Presence that abides with us in every aspect of our living, even through the moment of our physical death. There is an Egyptian proverb that reminds us that we have that Presence: "He who has no friend has God." There is Scripture's assurance, "And surely I am with you always, to the very end of the age" (Matthew 28:20).

That Presence is Father, Mother, Parent to us, a Being who loves us and is in control of all that over which we do not have power. It is One to whom we can go when we need help, when we do not know. It is a Source of reassurance to us in the face of all the mysteries that confound us. It is One that we can trust because that God is the Creator of our life, the One who sustains that life, and the ever-present Parent who has expressed unending love for us.

But to connect with this Parent we must be convinced of the reality of the spiritual realm and trust in the revelations that flow out of it into human history. When we admit who we really are and whence we have come, we can connect with that which is the Source of our being and all of which our life is part.

When we have been able to establish that honesty within ourselves, we will be positioned to be honest in our relationship with others and with the rest of the creation. Once we validate our own person in this way, who we are and the source of our life, we are affirmed as being important, worthy, acceptable, wanted, and loved by the Author of the whole eternal realm in which we live. Such affirmation is the architecture of healthy self-esteem.

From that base of self-assurance we no longer need pretend who we are, act through some false self that we erect to interact with our fellows. Having discarded the Great Lie, deceit need no longer be our tactic. We can act with confidence based on our honest feelings. We can risk sharing our genuine self with others, because even if we get hurt by doing that, we know we will not be destroyed. Our life has a dimension that goes beyond this physical existence and is in the care of a Spiritual

Power who is our loving Parent. In other words, we are freed from the need to masquerade. We can be "Real". As God's child, we can claim our inheritance.

CHAPTER 10: ACCEPTING

The journey we have made in this book is coming to its end. But life's journey, with which we have been dealing, will go on. From what we know through revelation, Scripture, human experience, and rational deduction, the creation is not a once-and-done thing. What we are a part of is a work in progress; we are participants in a developing phenomenon. As we direct our free will to be in union with the will of the system's Author, our life is designed to grow with the enterprise. All we need do is accept our birthright. But acceptance is not always easy, even of something we may appear to be eager to have. Consider the following.

A certain ruler came to Jesus asking, "Good teacher, what must I do to inherit eternal life?" The Teacher replied, "You know the commandments," and he enumerated some of them.

The ruler said, "All these I have kept since I was a boy." Then Jesus said to him, "You still lack one thing. Sell everything you have and give to the poor, and you will have great treasure in heaven. Then come, follow me. When he heard this he became very sad, because he was a man of great wealth" (Lu. 18: 18-23). It is hard for us to give up our wealth, even for something we may seem to want.

Money and possessions are not the only wealth that we can have. There is a richness that may come in the form of a way of life. Americans are blessed to live in a country that our founders felt was grounded in certain unalienable rights among which are "life, liberty and the pursuit of happiness." Our national anthem sings of "the land of the free and the home of the brave." We live in a society where the law seeks to preserve and protect innocent life. We are free, within social limits, to live according to our own conscience and pursue that which we may seek to make us happy and secure. And this is a wealth that God does not ask us to give up, but simply share in loving relationship.

But there is a danger inherent in a free and opulent society. The idea of individual freedom can be taken to excess. Freedom in the extreme is anarchy. In the pursuit of life, liberty, and happiness we are bound within the constraints of societal boundaries. We are also bound by the larger reality of which our life is part. We are not completely independent entities who can be the god of our own life. We cannot discard or ignore the spiritual element of our humanity and live as if physical reality is all there is. We are the children of a Higher Power and our contentment and fulfillment can come only as we acknowledge our fealty to that Being. We can achieve the fullness of our humanity only as we confess our need, our limitedness, and our vulnerability. It is this false idea of our individual sovereignty that God asks us to give up and "Then come, follow me."

INVITATION

Acceptance begins with an invitation. There is a rap on our door: "Here I am! I stand at the door and knock" (Rev.3:20). The response must be ours. We must open the door and welcome the One who is there. That act is an acknowledgment that we are in need of this Presence in our life, that we are limited, vulnerable, and dependent. In opening the door we declare the majesty of that which ordained life and we render our love in response to all we have received. And when we do that we are praying.

It is not necessary to kneel to pray. Prayer can be made at any time, in any place, from any position. Prayer is the gift of a channel for communication with that Power who is forming the creation. It is what we speak from the innermost place in our heart. Prayer opens our inner being to God, admitting the divine Power into our joys, our distress, our needs, our desires, our limitedness -- into our life. Prayer can be offered in joy, in thanksgiving, in tears, or in utter silence. Its mystery lies beyond the understanding of our finite minds. But its mystic process is a reality.

There is much misunderstanding about prayer, but in fact it is a very simple thing. We can talk to God about our needs and ask help with them, and this is legitimate - but God already knows our needs and wants to help us. We can legitimately pray for things that we want -- and God already knows about these also. It's okay to ask God's blessing on a particular undertaking - God wants to bless us in our honest endeavors. The fact is that God is fully acquainted with all our circumstances and it is His nature to act lovingly toward us.

So why should we pray at all if God is already disposed to us in these ways? We pray because in asking we honor Divine Love and acknowledge the grace we have received. All prayer should center about the fact that we could not exist outside of our Creator, nor could we continue to exist outside of Divine grace. God simply wants an invitation to come into our life and be there with us. "For thus says the high and lofty One who inhabits eternity, whose name is holy: 'I dwell in the high and holy place, and also with him who is of a contrite and humble spirit'" (Isa.57:15).

Our invitation, extended in humility and contrition, is a glorification of the Creator. It is the beginning of acceptance.

ACCEPTING THE GIFT OPENS THE GATE

If we have been foolish, we have not been abandoned by the Love which is the Parent of our life. Love reaches out to us, as we observed in Chapter Seven, to touch us, to reclaim us, to mend our brokenness, to heal our alienation, to make us real, to assure us of eternity. That voice, to which we may have said "no" for too long, is still calling out from beside the Galilean sea, "Come to me, all you who are weary and burdened, and I will give you rest" (Matthew 11:28).

It is the same voice that spoke to Abram in the land of Ur saying, "Leave your country, your people and your father's house and go to the land that I will show you. ...and all peoples on the earth will be blessed through you" (Gen. 12:1,3). Moses was called to the service of his people when he heard that voice say, "I have indeed seen the misery of my people in Egypt. I have heard them crying out... and am concerned about their suffering. So I have come down to rescue them..." (Ex. 3:7-8).

This is the voice that spoke to the people of Israel through the lips of the prophets. It is a voice that sings to all ages through the psalmists' prayers that bespeak every condition of our humanity. It is a voice that admonishes our foolishness, but invites us with Grace to become all that we were created to be.

It is the Word of which the evangelist John speaks when he proclaims that "the Word became flesh and made his dwelling among us" (John 1:14). This Word was a light to the world, teaching all who would listen that there is a different way to live together. Jesus of Nazareth, who is that Word embodied, brought to us a description of the kingdom of Love.

It is a kingdom that refutes and reverses the fallacies of the masquerade in which women and men have been engaged. It is a place that honors the meek, the merciful, the honest, those who seek righteousness, the peacemakers. It is a place where an enemy's broken humanity is recognized and foes are dealt with in compassion and concern. It is a place where the Creator of it all is the only recognized Sovereign. It is an eternal place. It is our place.

It is not a faraway place, distant in space or time, but a present reality if we care to open ourselves to it and accept it: "For if I drive out demons by the finger of God, then the kingdom of God has come to you" (Luke 11:20). In fact, what we discover when we honestly seek it is that we already have it, "because the kingdom of God is within you" (Luke 17:20-21).

It is not so much a place, but a condition of heart, soul, mind, and relationship. If we open our life to the Word, reconnect with the God who gave us life, admit that we are God's children, acknowledge our dependence, live in community, receive the Love that is offered, we find that Eden is real. It lies within the heart and mind of the seeker. Its gates open with the acceptance of the Love that created it.

RETURNING TO LOVE

It sounds so simple, doesn't it? Return to the Light! Return to the Parent who authored our life. Yet we find it so hard to make that surrender, for we are torn on the thorns of a dilemma we ourselves have created. Because we have lost the security that comes with connection with the Source of life, there is an uncertainty about where life is headed.

That makes us anxious and fearful. People are ill at ease. We fear death. The things of this world that we have sought after have brought us no assurance, no eternal peace. Trying to live the Great Lie has introduced a confusion and we have not been able to define who we really are. Therefore we have not been able to find peace within our own hearts, let alone be able to live in peace with each other. But despite this failure of our modus operandi, we have not faced up to the fallacy of the lie that we continue to pursue.

The lie has become endemic to our life, it has become an integral part of our culture. Patterson and Kim in their rigorous study of the minds of Americans, reported in their book *The Day America Told the Truth* that "we lie, and we don't even think about it. The people we lie to most are the people who are closest to us."[1] They found that 91 percent of us lie regularly.[2]

This cultural deceitfulness has its roots in the deception that occurs within our own personhood -- we have been lying to ourselves about who we are. The lie has led us to believe that we are what we are not. It gives us the illusion of mastery that we do not really have.

We are not gods, and no where does that become more evident than in our powerlessness to "come back home" on our own. Even the great apostle Paul had that trouble. He confessed in writing to the Romans, "For I have the desire to do what is good, but I cannot carry it out. For what I do is not the good I want to do; no, the evil I do not want to do -- this I keep doing" (Ro. 7:19).

And as a result of our self-deceit, we cannot apprehend the true nature of physical death. In the midst of our bent to be in control, we know deep within us that we cannot contain death. Since it is a discontinuance of our physical life, we fear death as an ending. We close our self off from the softer side of death: the miracle by which life transits from the physical to the spiritual. We lose the assurance that "he who believes has eternal life"(John 3:16).

But in this dilemma of our humanity, we find the saving hand of our Creator. It comes as a forgiving Grace that looks not on our fault but reads our heart. The truth was given to us by the Christ when he told us in his own words, "For God did not send his Son into the world to condemn the world, but to save the world through him" (John 3:17).

So if our heart is right with God and we are sincere in our desire, then we find that if our efforts do not reach perfection we will be forgiven "not seven times, but seventy times seven" (Matthew 12:22).

Patterson and Kim found that ninety percent of all Americans believe in God. But they also documented the fact that "fewer people are listening to what God has to say than ever before."[3] They found that people simply do not turn to God or religion to help them with seminal or moral issues of the day. Religion plays virtually no role in shaping our opinions on a long list of public questions. For most of us, God is a Being to be neither feared nor loved. From their data these investigators conclude, "Clearly, the God of the 1990's is a distant and pale reflection of the God of our forefathers."[4] In this chapter we are dealing with how to mend that relationship.

COVENANT

Relationships that are important to us are treated in special ways, some formal, others less so. Sometimes the terms of relationships are carefully spelled out in writing, while agreements on others may be sealed with a handshake. Some relationships like "best friends" require nothing more than an emotional bonding. Business agreements are almost always documented, even with the help of legal experts, so that all the details of the relationship are carefully enumerated. Other commitments, such as marriages, divorces, memberships, and so on, are also formalized in writing.

Symbols are also often a part of our being together in union. Organizations have "members only" jackets. We wear pins of various types to indicate our affiliations. We display or march under banners and flags; we have a national flag to which we "pledge allegiance." We have wedding bands, friendship jewelry, and class rings that symbolize our relationships.

These means that we use to document or declare or symbolize serve another important role in our associations. They not only record or display to others what it is that we are a part of, but they also stand as reminders to ourselves of those affiliations. A certificate of marriage and a wedding band tell us we are wife or husband. A uniform or badge tell the person who wears them who they are and what they represent. Written agreements help us remember that to which we gave assent; they can be referred to as the passage of time may require.

Symbols have a memory function; they remind us of who we are.

The cross, the crucifix, the sign of the fish, or the descending dove that many Christians display say something to others, but they also remind the wearer who she or he is. There are many other symbols and rituals that the church uses to remind it of what it is and from whence it came.

In God's relationship with humanity, God has used symbols as a means of identity and memory. As the Israelites wandered through the wilderness after escaping Egyptian bondage they were given a pillar of cloud to go before them in the daylight and a pillar of fire in the night - reminders of their God's presence with them (Ex.13:21). When God made covenant with Noah, God "set (His) rainbow in the clouds, and it will be a sign of the covenant between me and the earth" (Gen.9;12-13).

God has made covenant with those who come and renew their relationship with their Creator. "I will put my dwelling place among you... I will walk among you and be your God, and you will be my people" (Lev.26:11-12). For those of faith, God seals that covenant through a Divine act of which water is the symbol. It is called baptism. Baptism for virtually all Christians is God's act, the sign of the Creator's covenant. It gives birth to the cleansing transformation of life and a spiritual union bestowed as a Divine gift. It is mediated through the Son, in whom all things are brought together in unity (Col.1:17).

Baptism is a sacrament, an act in which the main action is taken by God. But there is also human activity in the event.

Participation in the ritual is a symbol of our devotion to that Source from whence life comes and through which life is sustained. The sign of this action is water. Water has been prominent throughout people's relationship with the Creator.

There were the waters over which God hovered in the act of creation. There were the waters that were parted as the Israelites fled their Egyptian captors. There were the floods in Noah's experience. There were the waters of the Jordan river in which Naaman was cleansed. And it was to these same waters that Jesus came to be baptized by John at the inauguration of His ministry. In the water of baptism, God brings to memory all of that history and seals the Divine covenant with us. We are united with our Creator, with each other, and with the creation of which we are part.

THE LOVE FEAST

The relationship thus renewed and sealed, we need to remain close to God to receive the nourishment that will sustain our authenticity as children of the Light. Jesus understood this need. As he was preparing to return to that realm from which he had come, he established a beautiful and simple way to provide for continued intimacy with us. He did it through the medium of a meal.

Basic to our physical life is the taking of nourishment for the body. Basic to our spiritual life is the taking of nourishment for the soul. Jesus invited those who would be children of God to break bread with him. "I stand at the door and knock. If anyone hears my voice and opens the door, I will come in and eat with him, and he with me" (Rev. 3:20).

What happens at this meal is a mysterious process, and its mechanics have been argued by people since Jesus invoked it with his disciples. Although we have no clue as to how it works, the Lord is present at that table. The story of two men of Emmaus demonstrates the reality of that Presence.

The two men were returning to their homes in Emmaus, a village about seven miles from Jerusalem. It was three days after Jesus had been crucified by the Romans. As they were walking, a third man joined them. While they walked, they discussed the recent events in Jerusalem. It was late in the day when they arrived at their village and they urged their new acquaintance, who appeared to be going to walk on, to stay with them for the night.

When they were about to eat their evening meal, the stranger took bread, as if he were the host, gave thanks, broke it, and passed it to them. Then, Scripture tells us, "their eyes were opened and they recognized him (Jesus), and he disappeared from their sight" (Luke 24:13-32).

Christians observe this breaking of bread together in what they know as the Lord's Supper. This Holy Communion recreates what Jesus told His disciples to do as an act of continuing relationship. It is an act of community; we do it together. In His last meal with them before his crucifixion Jesus "...took bread, and when he had given thanks, he broke it, and said, 'This is my body which is for you; do this in remembrance of me.' In the same way, after the supper, he took the cup saying, 'This cup is the new covenant in my blood; do this, whenever you drink it, in remembrance of me'" (1 Cor. 11:23-25).

In the solemn act of this holy meal, Christians experience the reality of the spiritual realm in their present physical world, for in this supper they apprehend the presence of their Lord. Kneeling in silent reverence they receive the spiritual nourishment that sustains them as they strive to become the persons they were created to be.

BE STILL AND KNOW

It is often in silence that we touch the spiritual. When we can cease our prattling, boasting, demanding, proclaiming, and striving we can be open to that which we have too long denied and ignored. The psalmist, ages ago, revealed that mystery to us in his song: "Be still before the Lord and wait patiently for him" (Ps. 37:07).

In the reverence of quietness we acknowledge our status before that Universal Consciousness that is the Parent of life. We respond to the truth of that which Israel was told: "Be still and know that I am God; I will be exalted among the nations, I will be exalted in the earth" (Ps. 46:10). It is then that we can rediscover an old truth, sung in an ancient psalm,

> I love you, O Lord, my strength.
> The Lord is my rock and fortress
> and my deliverer;

> my God is my rock, in whom I take refuge.
> He is my shield and the horn
> of my salvation, my stronghold.
> I call to the Lord, who is worthy
> of praise,
> and I am saved... (Psalm 18).

To know and experience that truth, to become "Real" once more, we must reach back through the clutter of duplicity with which we have deceived ourselves. We need to find again the original cloth from which we are made. For embedded in that fabric is the memory of an Eden-place. It is a memory we have lost, but not quite. It lies there at the core of our nature, waiting to rise again to the surface of our living. It is the remembrance of home, the place we wandered from in our prodigal's journey, the place to which we are meant to return.

But to go back home, to regain the ties of family and community that we have left, we must restore that archaic bond within which shalom was first experienced. We must connect again with the Parent whose house we left, because that attachment is the only source of true Love, agape.

In seeking that renewed relationship, we will discover the part of ourselves which humanity has long since renounced and discarded. It is the part that knows its place in the design of things. It is the part of us that can acknowledge we are child to the Parent, and can joyfully and thankfully experience that dependency. In this re-bonding with Love, we will know for certain who we are, whence we have come, and where we are going. We will find ourselves becoming all that we were created to be. We will have become who we really are, children of God.

And when we act from this authentic stance, we will no longer be caught in a state of alienation. Love is a connector that opens us to bonding relationship. When we are "real", we will find ourselves in harmonic community with God, with all other life, and with the creation of which we are this keystone piece. We will experience family in its fullest dimension. We will have discovered community. We will know the reality of heaven-on-earth.

SHALOM

There is an old story about a man who in the years of his living successfully made a journey to Eden. In closing I want to share it, for it shows how simple a thing it is to have what we have lost. In its simplicity it conveys a picture of soul-deep peace such that words alone cannot portray. It is a tableau of the contentment and assurance of a loving parent-child relationship. The story is from a little book titled *Beginning to Pray* by Anthony Bloom. The account is recorded from the life of a Catholic priest of France, the Cure d'Ars, Jean Marie Vianney.

It seems that there was an old peasant who used to come to the chapel each day and there he would spend hours, motionless, doing nothing. The priest observed this daily ritual. Finally, able to contain himself no longer, the curious cleric asked the peasant, "What is it that you do all these hours, sitting here in silence?" The old and worn man of the soil looked up at his priest and in a few simple words revealed the secret of his contentment. He said, "I look at Him, He looks at me, and we are happy."

It is my prayer that you too will know that deep inner contentment that the Hebrew names shalom.

NOTES

Chapter 1

1. Mitchell L. Gaynor, M.D. *Healing Essence* (New York: Kodansha America 1995) p.3
2. Ibid., p.14.
3. Ibid., p.15.
4. Ray S Anderson, *Don't Give Up On Me – I'm Not Finished* Yet (New York: Mc Kracken Press, 1994), p6.
5. Bruce C. Birch, *To Love As We Are Loved* (Nashville, Tn.: Abington Press, 1992), p.3.
6. Ibid., p.17.
7. Ibid., p.36.
8. Ibid., p.57.
9. From "Guess What... God Knows Best" by Glen T Stanton, *Focus On The Family*, August 1995, p.3.
10. Ibid., p.3.
11. Ibid., p.3.
12. Ibid., p.4.
13. Ibid., p.4.

Chapter 2

1. Gary Smalley and John Trent, *The Blessing* (New York: Simon and Schuster Inc., 1986)
2. Quoted in *Alive Now*, Nov/Dec. 1991, p.4.
3. M. Scott Peck, M.D., *The Different Drum* (New York, Simon and Schuster, 1987), p.193

4. Quoted in *Alive Now*, Op.Cit., p.12.
5. James Patterson and Peter Kim, *The Day America Told The Truth* (New York: Simon and Schuster, 1991), p.239.
6. Ibid., p.236
7. Ibid., p.172
8. Paul Huber, *Creation for What?* (New York: Vantage Press, Inc., 1988), p.151.

Chapter 3

1. M. Scott Peck, M.D., *The Road Less Traveled* (New York: Simon and Schuster, 1978),pp.208-210.
2. Lewis Thomas, *The Lives of a Cell* (New York: Bantam Books, 1974), p.145.
3. Ibid.,m p.147.
4. Ibid., p.33.
5. From "Inside the Mind of John Wheeler" by J. Boslough, *The Readers' Digest*, Sept. 1986, pp. 106-110.
6. Thomas, *The Lives*, p.167.

Chapter 4

1. Huber, *Creation*, p.8.
2. Ibid., p.33.
3. See A. Richardson, Ed., *A Dictionary of Christian Theology* (Philadelphia: The Westminster Press, 1969), p. 140.

4. Stephen W. Hawking, *A Brief History of Time*, (New York: Bantam Books, 1988) p. 122.
5. Huber, *Creation*, pp. 51-52.
6. Hawking, *A Brief*, p.127
7. See Mark 10:6; 13:9
8. Quoted in Ram Dass and Paul Gorman, How Can I Help? (New York: Knopf, 1987).
9. Lewis, *the Lives*, p.122.
10. Carlo Carreto, *Why O Lord?* (Maryknoll, New York:Orbis Books, 1986) p.36.

Chapter 5

1. Dyson, *Living*, pp. 48-50.
2. Eric Berne, *A Layman's Guide to Psychiatry and Psychoanalysis* (New York: Simon and Schuster, 1968), p. 88.
3. Peck, *The Road*, pp. 239-240.

Chapter 6

1. Merlin Carothers, *Prison to Praise* (Escondido, Calif.: Merlin R. Carothers, 1970, p.14.

Chapter 7

1. Melvin Morse, M.D. with Paul Perry, *Transformed by the Light* (New York: Villard Books, 1992), p. 17.

2. Joan W. Anderson, *Where Angles Walk* (Carmel, N.Y.: Guidposts, 1992), pp.55-57.

Chapter 8

1. Melvin Morse, M.D. with Paul Perry, *Closer to the Light* (New York: Villard Books, 1990), p. 120.
2. Huber, *Creation*, p. 9.
3. Hawking, *A Brief*, p.127.
4. Huber, *Creation*, p.18.
5. Morse, *Closer To*, p.75.
6. Dyson, *Living*, pp. 44-45.
7. Morse, *Closer To*, pp. 169-171.
8. Dyson, *Living*, pp. 118-119.
9. Bernie S. Siegel, M.D., *Love, Medicine and Miracles* (New York: Harper and Row Publishers, 1986), p. 181.

Chapter 9

1. Carretto, *Why*, p.88.
2. Ibid., p.55.
3. Quoted in *Live Now*, Op. Cit., pp. 26-27.

Chapter 10

1. Patterson and Kim, *The Day*, p.236
2. Ibid., p.45
3. Ibid., p. 199.
4. Ibid., p. 201.

Made in the USA
Lexington, KY
27 December 2012